SMOCKING

EMBROIDERY · SKILLS

SMOCKING

Anne Andrew

MEREHURST
—— LONDON ——

Published 1989 by Merehurst Press
Ferry House
51–57 Lacy Road
Putney
London SW15 1PR

Reprinted 1990
© Copyright 1989 Merehurst Limited
ISBN 1 85391 060 0

Edited by Diana Brinton
Designed by Bill Mason
Photography by Stewart Grant (page 94 by
Mary Fortune)
Drawings by Lindsay Blow
Typesetting by Rowland Phototypesetting Limited,
Bury St Edmunds, Suffolk
Colour Separation by Scantrans Pte Limited, Singapore
Printed in Italy by
New Interlitho SpA, Milan

Distributed by
STERLING PUBLISHING CO., INC.
387 Park Avenue South
New York, N. Y. 10016-8810

CONTENTS

INTRODUCTION

The word smocking describes the decorative stitchery which was used to control gathers on the loose-fitting, traditional blouse, called the smock (this was an old English word for chemise or shift). Although there is evidence that a form of smocking was sometimes used on the dress of the wealthy as far back as the 15th century, the principal era of smocks belongs to the late 17th and 18th centuries. This decorative but practical garment was worn by most agricultural workers and children in England and Wales during this period. With the coming of mechanization, the loose garment became impractical and its use gradually died out, but the skills of smocking were transferred to the decoration of ladies' and children's wear, and in the early part of the 20th century, the technique became very fashionable. Two world wars brought many social changes and the labour-intensive hand smocking was overtaken by cheaper mass production for adults' clothes. However, the skills of smocking continued, mainly as decoration on children's garments.

In recent years there has been a great surge of interest in the use of embroidery in a free and experimental form. Students and embroidery enthusiasts are looking at all forms of the art as a way of expressing their own ideas and feelings. The traditional image of smocking has been slow to change, but its adaptability is now being recognized and appreciated. As an interpretative medium, it has endless potential for inclusion in embroidery panels and hangings, as well as being a method of providing richly decorative texture for fashion garments. As with any other technique, the basic knowledge is essential to give you confidence to progress to a more experimental form if you wish. This book aims to give you that confidence, by taking you through the basic steps, and then encouraging you to develop your own ideas and designs.

This modern dress version of a traditional labourer's smock is made in silk. The smock was designed and stitched to commission by the author, and the box embroidery on each side of the smocking incorporates the three-crown symbol and stylized initials of Coutts Bank (photographed by kind permission of Mrs Penny Money Coutts).

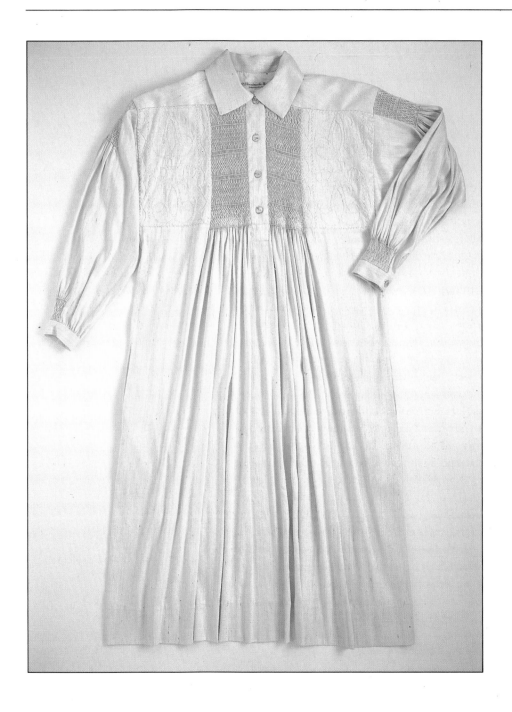

CHAPTER 1

SMOCKING BASICS

Materials and equipment

Fabrics

Although the vast choice of fabrics available today can be quite bewildering, it is also very exciting. New fabrics are constantly being created, and the colours, textures, richness and delicacy are an inspiration to dressmakers and embroiderers alike.

The traditional natural fabrics for smocking are still available, and cottons, linens, wools and silks will always be popular. However, mixtures of these with man-made fibres combine the practicality of easy care and crease resistance with the properties of the natural fibres. For instance, polyester/cotton mixtures are ideal for children's clothes, because they wear well and wash easily. Cotton, cotton lawn, wool/cotton mixtures and fine denim also smock well.

Care needs to be taken when choosing fabrics to smock for adult clothes. As well as being suitable for the style, a fabric must hang and drape well, to avoid too much bulk. Polyester cottons, pure cottons, silks, wool crêpe, challis and fine jersey all smock beautifully. Chiffon, crêpe de chine, georgette, velvet and loose knitted fabrics are more difficult to handle, but will give lovely results for the more experienced smocker.

Whichever fabric you choose, make sure it is of good quality. There is a temptation, when starting out, to buy a cheap fabric so as not to waste money. This is always a false economy – you will be disappointed with the result, because a poor fabric does not show your smocking to advantage and will not do justice to the time and effort you have spent on it. Good quality fabric does not need to be expensive, and there are plenty of cottons, as well as mixtures of polyester with either cotton or wool, all of which are suitable for smocking. The fabric should be evenly woven and have enough weight to hang well, and when gathered, the folds should have a rounded shape, providing a good base for your smocking stitches.

A selection of fabrics suitable for smocking: silk dupion, velvet, dress-weight cotton, lawn, calico, rayon, silk habutai, gingham, jersey, wool challis and polyester/cotton (from top to bottom). The threads should be chosen to complement the type and weight of fabric; those shown here include various weights of silk, Danish flower threads, perlé and stranded cottons, and coton á broder.

Gathering threads

These are used to gather the fabric and pull it up into pleats, ready for smocking. Good quality cotton thread or polyester/cotton No. 40 are suitable for most fabrics, but if you are smocking a heavy-weight fabric you may need to use buttonhole twist or quilting thread for extra strength. The gathering threads form the guidelines for your smocking stitches, so choose a colour that contrasts with your fabric.

Embroidery threads

Any good quality embroidery thread can be used for smocking, as long as its weight is in proportion to that of the fabric. Suitable threads include stranded cotton, coton à broder, perlé cotton and soft cotton, all of which are readily available in a good range of colours. Stranded cotton is a six-stranded cotton with a good sheen. Coton à broder is a very smooth shiny single-strand cotton, available in a variety of thicknesses; No. 25 is the finest, but you will also find 20, 16 and 12. Perlé cotton is a twisted cotton with a sheen; Nos 3 and 5 are available in skeins and No. 8 (the finest) in balls. Soft cotton is a thick mat embroidery thread.

Danish flower threads are also useful. These are fine dull cotton threads in lovely natural colours. Silk threads may be either stranded or twisted and are available in a range of thicknesses. Linen threads come in a good range of colours – if you can find them. They are twisted, have a sheen, and are very strong. Rayon threads may be either stranded or twisted and are very shiny, catching the light beautifully, but they are rather springy to sew with. Crochet cotton is a rather hard thread, but available in a range of weights.

Knitting yarns in wool, cotton or lurex are all worth trying. For more experimental work, cotton and rayon tapes, ribbons, metallic threads, and space-dyed threads produce very interesting results.

Needles

Crewel needles with a long eye are ideal for smocking. Sizes 7, 8 or 9 are the most useful, but try out different sizes before you start. The needle must be large enough to be threaded easily, without splitting the thread, and it should pass through the fabric easily, without leaving a large hole.

Preparing the fabric

The folds or pleats on which the smocking stitches are worked are formed by rows of gathering stitches, placed exactly above one another. In the past, this was done by eye, but now there are various methods to help mark the fabric. These mark the picking up points for the gathering threads and must be placed accurately on the straight grain of the fabric so that the pleats fall straight and parallel.

Care in preparation at this stage is essential and will result in a beautifully gathered piece of fabric. This is part of the charm of smocking, as well as a basis for your stitches. Press the fabric well, so that there are no creases to distort the placing of the dots.

Smocking dot transfers

These are ironed on the fabric and are sold, in a variety of sizes, in sheets about 18cm (7in.) deep and 90cm (36in.) wide. The size you

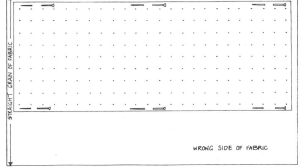

1 To make sure that your fabric has been cut on the straight grain, pull out a weft thread along the top edge. If there is any distortion, use this line as a guide when cutting away surplus fabric.

2 To use transfer dots, first test on a spare piece of fabric, then cut a transfer sheet to the correct size and place it, wax side down, on the wrong side of the fabric. Align it with the straight grain, and allow an extra row of dots at the top and bottom – these will give you greater control when you stitch. Pin the sheet in place; press the iron firmly over it; raise it, then place it on the next section. Do not rub the iron or the dots will be smudged. Lift a corner and check that the dots have transferred before you remove the sheet.

use depends on the fabric: fine fabrics need shallow folds and therefore closely placed dots; widely placed dots make deeper folds, and allow for the bulk of heavier fabrics. As a general guide, dots 6mm (¼in.) apart are ideal for polyester/cotton or lawn. Cut off the manufacturer's name to use for testing on a small piece of your fabric, in order to determine the lowest heat setting at which your iron will transfer the dots clearly. Too hot a setting will make the dots show on the right side, and may distort a man-made fabric. Place the test piece of transfer face down on the wrong side of the fabric and iron firmly. Check also at this stage that the transfer dots will wash out, then mark the main fabric.

Tissue paper

This method is the best for fine, delicate fabrics, through which the transfer dots would be visible, or for patterned materials on which the dots would not show. Mark the dot pattern on tissue paper, using a sheet of transfer dots as a guide. Baste the tissue paper firmly to the wrong side of the fabric, taking care to align the dots with the straight grain. Using the gathering thread, pick up the tissue and fabric together at each dot and gently pull the tissue away when all the gathering is complete.

Water- and air-soluble pens

Semi-transparent materials can be marked with either a water- or air-soluble pen, both of which look like felt tip pens. The dots marked with the water-soluble pen can be sponged away gently with a damp cloth after the gathering has been completed. The dots marked with the air-soluble pen will disappear within 24 hours, so gathering must be completed as soon as possible after marking. This pen is invaluable for marking silk fabric, which might be stained by water.

Mark the wrong side of the fabric, following the straight grain. Use a ruler or a sheet of smocking dots as a guide. The rows of dots are repeated evenly and are spaced to the required depth. Another method is to baste a sheet of smocking dots to the right side of the fabric; hold it up against a window or over glass with a light underneath, so that the dots show through the fabric, then mark the dots on the wrong side.

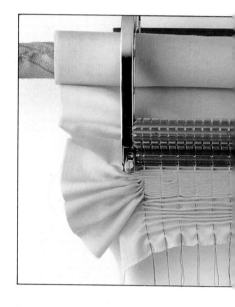

A smocking machine is useful for gathering, particularly if you are making children's clothes in large quantities. The chief disadvantage of smocking machines (apart from the price) is that the depth of gathering is limited by the width of the rollers.

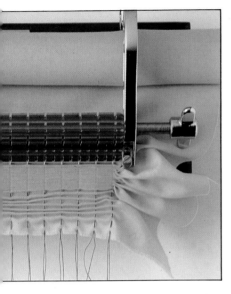

Gathering the fabric

When the dots have been marked, the fabric can then be gathered, either by hand, as shown (1, 2), or by machine. The latter is available in two widths and has a series of needles that are threaded with cotton and are set between rotating rollers. As the fabric is fed through the machine it is gathered to the required depth.

The machine does, however, have some limitations: only light-weight fabrics can be used, and the pleat depth is set at approximately 6mm (¼in.) and cannot be varied. It requires some skill to feed the fabric through the rollers, keeping the grain straight right across the piece of fabric, although this can be helped by rolling the fabric around a thick dowel first. For experimental work, when the position of the straight grain is not so vital, a machine can be used very successfully. It is also ideal for someone who does a great deal of smocking on light-weight fabrics, or for a group of people to share.

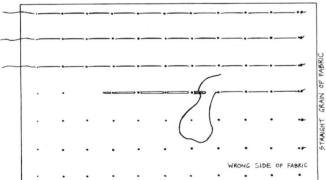

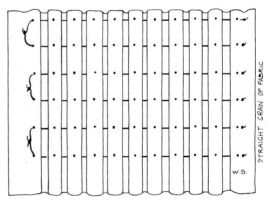

1 Use a contrasting thread, a little longer than the width of the fabric. Make a firm knot at one end and, working on the wrong side of the fabric, start with a small back stitch at the first dot, to hold the thread securely when you gather. Pick up a small amount of fabric at each dot and work across the row, leaving the thread hanging loose at the end. After a little practice, you can pick up several stitches on the needle before pulling the thread through. Continue across each row in turn.

2 When all the rows are complete, hold the thread ends and gently ease the fabric along the threads, forming the folds. Pull the fabric lengthwise every so often, to help to set the pleats. If there is any puckering, pull the fabric lengthwise again and stroke along the pleats with a blunt needle. Wrap pairs of threads around a pin to hold them until you are ready to smock. Then undo the pins, and ease the pleats out to a little less than the required finished length. You should be able to see the gathering threads between the pleats. Knot the threads in pairs.

CHAPTER 2

STITCHES AND VARIATIONS

Starting the smocking

The elasticity of smocking is one of its main properties, and helps to make garments comfortable and easy to wear. The stitches not only form a highly decorative surface and control the pleats, but their shape allows them to stretch slightly.

Not all embroidery stitches are suitable: some hold the pleats too tightly and will not allow any movement. All smocking patterns are based on the following stitches, and it is best to work a sampler of each stitch first. This will not only help you to learn the stitch, but it will also allow you to build up a rhythm of working. Choose a colour of fabric that pleases you and a colour of thread that contrasts well, so that the stitches stand out clearly, and the samplers can act as your reference notebook.

You will soon see that the stitches vary in the amount of control that they offer, and that tension is as important in smocking as in knitting. The correct tension will come with practice: too loose a tension will result in untidy stitches, and the pleats will not hold in position; too tight a tension will make the stitches look flat, and will hold the pleats so tightly that there is no movement. Try to achieve even stitches that are nicely rounded and show their shape well. It should be possible to pull the completed piece of work out easily, and it should then spring back into shape when released.

All smocking stitches are worked from left to right, except van-dyke and feather stitch. With the exception of trellis and wave stitch, the needle is always at right angles to the pleat. The position of the thread – whether it is placed above or below the needle when you make each stitch – governs the shape and position of the stitch. You will soon recognize when the shape of the stitch is wrong, and you will find that it is usually the position of the thread that is at fault. With practice, it will become automatic to place the thread correctly.

This child's winter dress is made of vyella and smocked, from the yoke to the waist and around the sleeves, in tones of pale pink.

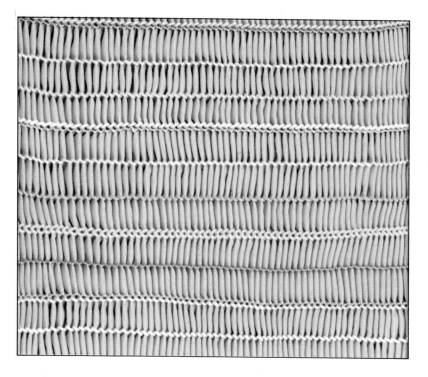

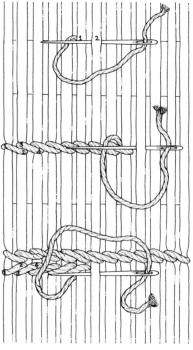

Outline stitch (1)

This is also known as rope stitch and was widely used on the old smocks. It is worked in the same way as stem stitch, in surface embroidery, and is a useful first stitch in a design because it holds the pleats firmly. It forms a continuous rolled line that can be used to outline other stitches.

Other rows can be added to the first, perhaps with the spacing between them varied, to suit the design. When a second row of this stitch is placed just under the first, the thread may be kept above the needle, reversing the stitch to form a wheatear or mock chain stitch.

1 To make a row of outline stitching, take approximately 45cm (18in.) of thread and make a knot at one end. Bring the needle up through the left-hand side of the first pleat, level with a row of gathering threads. Keeping the thread below the needle, push the needle into the right-hand side of the next pleat and at right angles to it. Bring it out on the left side, picking up the top third of the pleat. Continue in the same way, picking up each pleat in turn. Keep a straight line, using the gathering threads as a guide. When you reach the end, push the needle down beside the last pleat and fasten off with two or three back stitches on the back of the pleat.

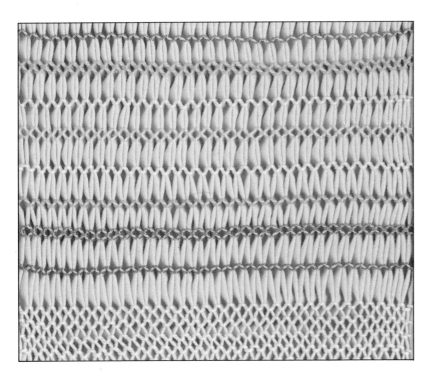

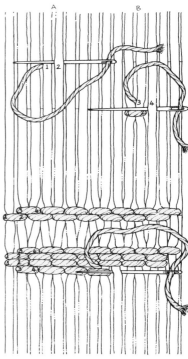

Cable stitch (2)

This is worked in the same way as outline stitch, but it appears different because the thread is placed alternately above and below the needle. This is a firm stitch and, like outline stitch, it is a useful way of holding the pleats at the start of a pattern. It can be repeated in spaced rows, and was used in this way on many of the old smocks. It forms an interesting texture, rather like purl knitting, and it can look very effective when the thread has been chosen to match the fabric.

Double cable

Two rows of cable stitch, worked close together, make a double cable, looking rather like the links of a chain. The second row is an exact reverse of the first, so if you started the first row with the thread below the needle, start the first stitch of the second row with the thread above the needle. The stitches should lie neatly together, alternately touching and then leaving a space.

2 For cable stitch, start off as for outline, taking the first stitch with the thread below the needle (A). Next, place the thread above the needle and take the second stitch (B). Keep your needle at right angles to the pleats, and maintain a straight line across the work, picking up each pleat in turn. The stitches should be rounded and should sit neatly, lying alternately above and below each other. Learn to recognize the shape of the stitch, and you will soon see if you have made a mistake, forgetting to change the position of the thread with each stitch.

17

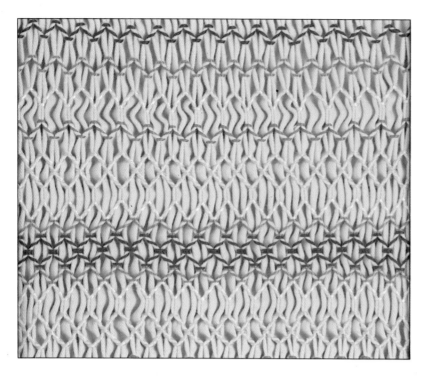

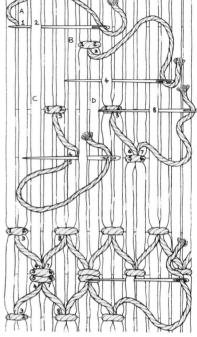

Diamond stitch (1)

This is a very versatile stitch, which can be used in blocks, and works well with other stitches. It can also be overlapped, as will be shown later. The instructions describe how to make one half of the stitch, and this can be used on its own, in spaced rows. The diamond is formed by making a second row, reversing the stitch.

This is a quick stitch to work and its wide spacing makes it very elastic. Beware of making the diamond stitches too large, as will be the case if your gathering rows are more than 12mm (½in.) apart. If this is so, work the complete diamond between the two rows of gathering threads, bringing the needle down at B to half way between the two rows.

1 Diamond stitch is worked using two rows of gathering stitches as guidelines. Bring the thread out to the left of the first pleat. Put the needle through the next pleat (A), keeping the needle horizontal, with the thread above it, as for cable stitch. The next stitch is taken on a level with the lower gathering thread: keeping the thread above the needle and the needle horizontal, take a stitch through the next pleat (B). Next, place the thread below the needle and take a stitch into the adjacent pleat, as for cable stitch (C). With the thread still below the needle, take a stitch into the next pleat, level with the top row of gathering threads (D).

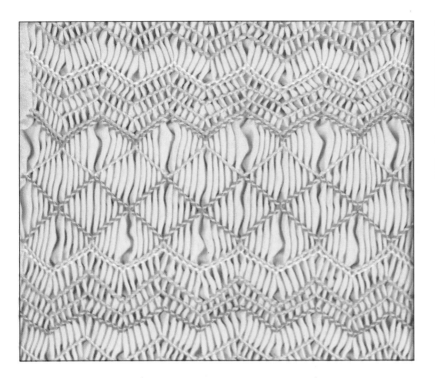

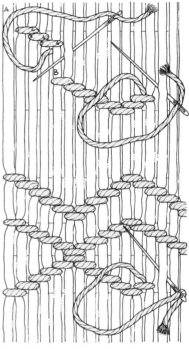

Wave and trellis stitch (2)

This is worked diagonally in steps down and up between two rows of gathering threads. To keep the stitches lying straight across the pleats, the needle is angled down when working down and up when working up. As a result, the stitches are stacked step by step. If the needle were to be kept straight when making this stitch, the thread would finish at an angle to the pleats.

The instructions describe how to make one row of wave stitch. The rows can be spaced apart or set close together, which makes a much bolder wave. This can look very attractive, if you use a succession of threads in tones of the same colour.

Trellis stitch is formed by reversing the process, creating a row of diamond shapes. These can stand on their own or in combination with wave stitch, and are used effectively in many designs. This is a stitch that takes some practice to perfect, but it is well worth the effort.

2 To make wave stitch, start by bringing the needle up on the left-hand side of the first pleat. Keeping the thread up, take a stitch into the next pleat at the same level, but with the needle angled slightly downward. Continue to stitch in this way, making sure that you keep the stitches even, until you reach the lower gathering thread (A). Keeping the thread down, take the next stitch with the needle angled slightly upward. Continue to work up, making the same number of stitches as were made on the way down and keeping them even (B).

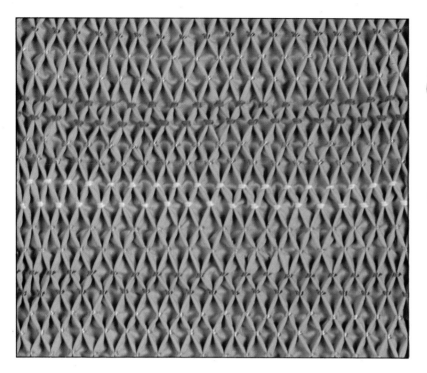

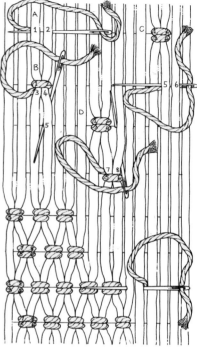

Honeycomb stitch 1

As its name implies, this stitch creates a texture that resembles the cells of a bee hive. Because there is very little surface stitchery, honeycomb has a delicate appearance, and it is very elastic. Like diamond stitch, it is worked between two rows of gathering threads or, if the gap between the rows is too large, you can take the stitches to a point halfway between the rows. After you have made the first row, the second and subsequent rows are worked in the same way, building up the characteristic cell structure.

1 Keep the thread above or below the needle, according to the diagram. **Bring the needle out on the left of the first pleat, at right angles to it; stitch into the second pleat and through to the left side of the first, pulling them together (A). Insert the needle into the right side of the second pleat; angle it down under the fabric, bringing it out at the left side of the second pleat, level with the lower gathering row (B). Stitch through the third and second pleats (C). Insert the needle into the right side of the third pleat and angle it up behind the fabric and out on the left side of the third pleat, level with the top gathering row (D).**

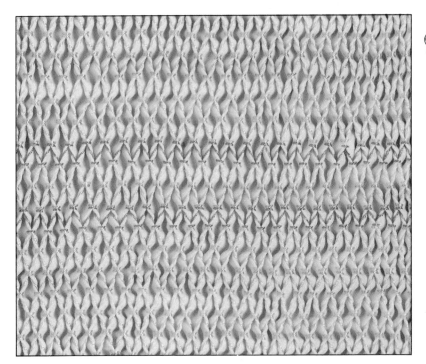

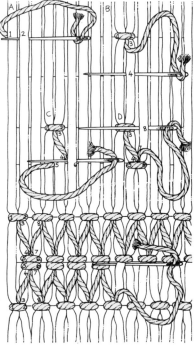

Surface honeycomb 2

All the stitchery is on the front of the fabric when you use surface honeycomb: the pleats are stitched across, as with cable stitch, but they are also wrapped with thread, resulting in a highly textured surface. If you follow the first row by stitching the second row in reverse, a wrapped diamond shape will result.

Surface honeycomb is worked in almost the same way as diamond stitch, and consequently the two are sometimes confused. As with diamond stitch and honeycomb, use two rows of gathering threads as guides, or stitch to a point halfway between the rows. The difference between diamond and surface honeycomb is that in the latter case, the stitch is taken over the same pleat, wrapping it with thread.

2 Begin surface honeycomb by bringing the needle out on the left-hand side of the first pleat, in line with the top gathering thread. Keeping the thread above the needle and the needle at right angles to the pleat, pick up a stitch on the second pleat, as for cable stitch (A). Take another stitch on the second pleat, again with the thread above the needle, but this time at the lower level (B). Take a stitch through the third pleat, with the thread below the needle (C). Keeping the thread below the needle, take another stitch through the third pleat, but at the top level of gathering threads (D). Continue across the row.

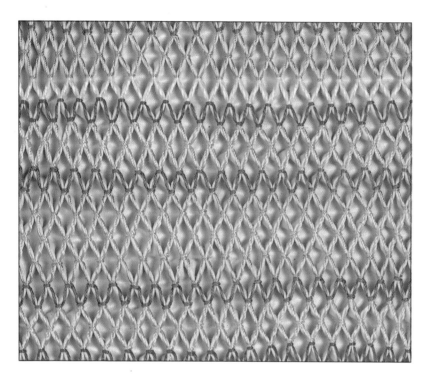

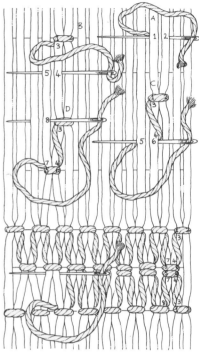

Vandyke stitch (1)

This stitch is worked from right to left. The thread is wrapped around the pleats, as in surface honeycomb, but as it is worked in a different direction the resulting cell shape has a slightly square appearance. Vandyke stitch can be used on its own, in spaced rows, or you can work a second row in reverse, to form a square, wrapped shape.

1 Keep the thread above or below the needle, according to the diagram. Bring the thread up on the left side of the second pleat from the right end of the work. With the needle horizontal, backstitch through the first and second pleats (A). Drop to the lower gathering row; insert the needle into the right side of the second pleat and through the third, wrapping the second (B). Backstitch through the second and third pleats (C). Wrap the third pleat by inserting the needle into the right side of the third pleat, level with the top gathering row, and through to the fourth pleat. Backstitch these pleats together and continue to the end of the row (D).

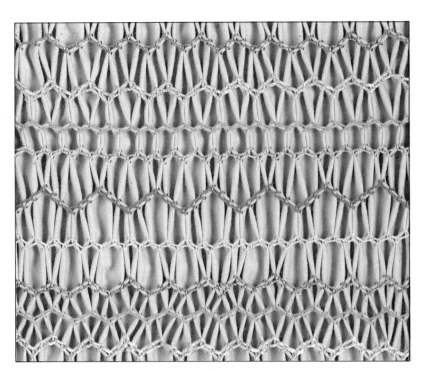

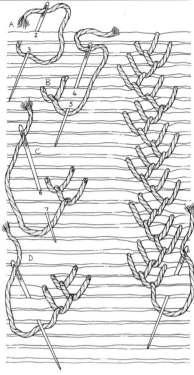

Feather stitch (2)

In pictures of old smocks, you will see this stitch used extensively to form the patterns that decorate the boxes, collars and yokes. It can also be used as a smocking stitch, in which case it is worked in just the same way as on flat fabric.

The stitch is formed with a loop, as with blanket stitch, and it changes direction from side to side, with either one, two or three stitches each way, to create a pretty zigzag line. For a wider zigzag, three stitches each side can be taken, or for a narrower line, just one stitch each side. Try to keep the stitches evenly spaced and the tension constant throughout. This is a light, delicate stitch, contrasting well with the more geometric shapes of the other smocking stitches. In the diagram, the stitch is worked over two pleats at a time, but for a more elastic stitch you can work over one pleat at a time.

2 Turn the fabric so that the pleats lie horizontally, and stitch towards you. Bring the needle up under the first pleat, then swing the thread down and to the right. Holding the thread with your thumb, take a stitch to the right, through the first and second pleats. Bring the needle out over the thread, forming a loop (A). Take the next stitch in the same way, through the second and third pleats, making a step to the right (B). Now swing the thread down and to the left, and take the next stitch to the left, forming a loop as before (C). Continue, taking two stitches to the left and right in turn, dropping one pleat each time (D).

Stitch sampler

Having worked samples of the basic stitches, the next stage is to use some of them together to make up a design. Choose an attractive colour for your background fabric and cut a piece 23cm (9in.) deep by approximately 60cm (24in.). Mark it with 13 rows of dots 12mm (½in.) apart. Gather with a contrasting thread and pull the rows up, ready for smocking. You will need four colours of embroidery thread for this design. Choose a colour scheme that blends well, but that also shows up clearly against the background. A useful combination is three tones of one colour, plus a contrast colour, as used in the photograph.

When starting a new piece of smocking, it is advisable to try out a few stitches of each row first, to see how the design is working out. This saves having to undo a complete row if a mistake has been made, or if you wish to adjust the order of stitches or change the colours. In the sample shown here, instructions are given for each stage and for the order of colours, but as you become more confident you will want to develop your own ideas. Follow the chart and colour layout and refer back to the stitch diagrams, if necessary.

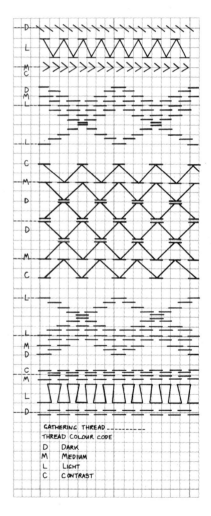

Each vertical line on the chart represents one pleat, and the stitches are shown in diagrammatical form. The rows of gathering thread are indicated to the left of the chart: leave a row at the top and bottom of your sampler to make it easier to control the pleats as you work.

The stitches are all worked either in line with a row of gathering threads or halfway between two rows. These rows are clearly shown on the chart, to help you with the spacing of the stitches.

Vandyke stitch, used at the bottom of the design, is worked from right to left. As it is easier to start all the rows from the same edge, turn your fabric upside down when you reach this stage, so that you can start the vandyke stitch from the same side as all the other rows.

From top to bottom, the stitches used are as follows. Outline, surface honeycomb, double outline, wave, trellis, diamond, trellis, wave, double cable, vandyke, and cable.

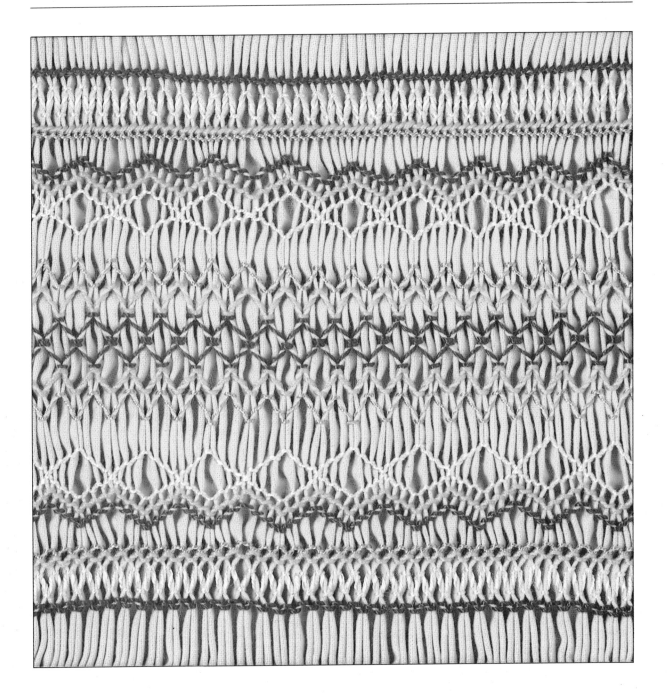

Finishing and stretching

When you have completed a smocking pattern, place the smocked fabric face down on an ironing board and pin it in position, keeping the pleats straight. Using a steam iron or a dry iron and a damp cloth, steam the smocking to set the pleats and stitches, holding the iron just above the fabric. Never press the smocking, or the pleats will flatten and be distorted. Leave the piece to dry completely; then unpin it, and remove the gathering threads.

If the smocking is to be set into a garment, leave the top gathering thread in place, as this helps to control the pleats while you are making it up. Sometimes the smocking may seem a little too tight to fit into position in a garment, but it can be stretched slightly: remove the gathering threads and pull out the smocking gently and evenly to the required width. Pin the smocked fabric to an ironing board, pulling the pleats straight. Steam the smocking as before and leave it to dry, when it should retain the correct width.

A finished piece of smocking is pinned, right side down, to an ironing board. The steam from the iron, which is held just above the fabric, helps to set the pleats.

A variety of stitches, in a charming colour scheme formed from shades of pink and blue, has been used to smock this pale blue dress, by Hilary Christie. The smocking is decorated with a scattering of embroidered flowers. The pink smocking is echoed on the scalloped edging around the collar and sleeves.

If the tension of the stitches is too tight to allow much movement, you will not be able to stretch the work, even by steaming, without distorting the pleats. For this reason, always make a tension sample before embarking on a large piece of work. A heavy concentration of stitches may also hold the pleats tightly, so try to space the rows of stitches, in order to allow adequate elasticity.

Patterns

The patterns of smocking are built up by choosing stitches in relation to one another, by stitch variations, and by combinations of the stitches. You will see from the samples that the straight-line stitches – outline and cable – create a definite division across the design. Diamond, surface honeycomb, vandyke, wave and trellis stitches, all of which form zigzag shapes, lend themselves to geometric and diagonal designs. The softer shape of feather stitch and the dainty honeycomb can be used to create a lighter effect.

In addition to the appearance, bear in mind the elasticity of the stitches. It may be that a complex and elaborate pattern will create too firm a fabric for your purposes, especially if it contains large blocks of cable.

When planning a design, it helps to keep these characteristics in mind, and to note how one stitch falls naturally into shape with another, especially when you use zigzag stitches. The scope for more creative ideas is greater than it might at first appear, because nearly all the stitches can be varied. You may decide to change the scale and depth of the stitch, or to put in an extra step. You may choose to build stitches up into blocked shapes, or to overlay and cross stitches. Once you start to think in this way, numerous design possibilities are opened up.

Diamond stitch (1, 2, 3, 4, 5)
The variations that are shown here, in chart form on graph paper, give just an idea of the way in which diamond stitch can be adapted, using long and short stitches, overlapping, and taking extra steps or individual stitches.

Surface honeycomb (6) *and vandyke*
The variations that are shown here for diamond stitch can, with the exception of the third example, be applied to both honeycomb and vandyke stitches. If you take a sheet of graph paper and some coloured pencils, you will be able to discover many more variations for yourself. Bear in mind, when experimenting with graph patterns, that vandyke is worked from right to left.

Diamond stitch

Surface honeycomb

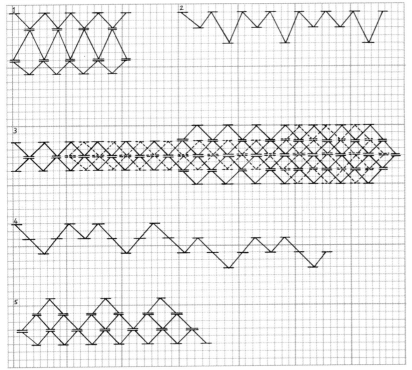

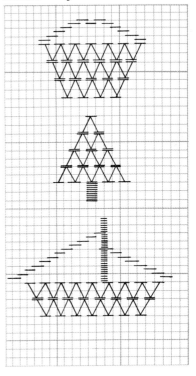

1 If you alternate rows of long and short stitches, you can make elongated diamond shapes.

2 Long and short stitches may be used in the same row in a range of combinations.

3 As diamond is a wide stitch, leaving two pleats between the top and bottom stitches, it is possible to overlap one row with another, perhaps using a contrast colour.

4 Here, the pattern is formed by adding an extra step. Refer back to the stitch diagram on page 18 and, at stage C, take the straight part of the stitch from 5 to 6 with the thread up, then take another stitch down to the next pleat, as in stage B. This makes a much deeper stitch, and one that is considerably lighter and more elastic.

5 Single diamond stitches (along the top row) may be used to complete a triangular pattern. Work each stitch separately, starting and finishing individually.

6 Surface honeycomb may be worked in blocks, which can be shaped into simple motifs, such as a tree, a basket or a boat. Rather than stitching each row of the shape separately, make the first row in the normal way, then pass the needle through to the back of the fabric. Turn the work around, from top to bottom, and bring the needle up to the front again, ready to start the next row. To make the shape, start one pleat in from the last stitch to decrease the size or one pleat out to increase it. Finish the shape, turning between rows, and fasten off.

Wave and trellis stitch (1)

The number of steps taken up and down with this stitch can be altered to offer a vast range of variations. Patterns with different sizes of zigzags can be built up, rather like Florentine stitch in canvas embroidery. The rows may be worked close together or spaced apart, and all can be crossed over each other or joined to form diamond shapes.

Cable stitch (2, 3, 4)

The plain, straight cable stitch reveals a surprising versatility once you begin to experiment, and can be built up into a wide number of images and patterns. While exploring all these variations, however, take care to ensure that the gaps between stitches are never so big as to leave loops of thread that might catch easily. There is also a danger of concentrating the stitches together to such an extent that the smocking loses its elasticity.

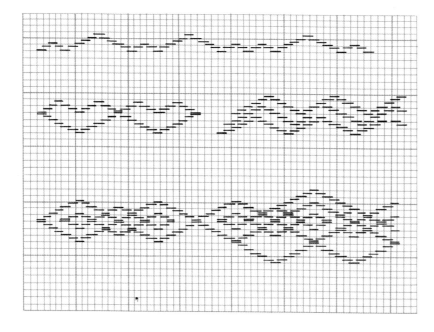

1 Here are just a few of the innumerable variations that can be achieved with wave and trellis stitch; but try doodling some patterns of your own on graph paper and see how easily they can be interpreted in wave and trellis.

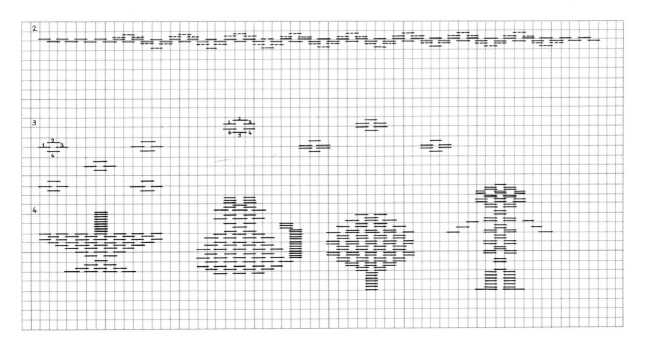

2 The straight line of cable stitch is here softened by the addition of groups of three extra stitches, set alternately on either side of the row. Work a row of single cable first; then take a new thread and stitch three cables above and close to the first row, as for double cable. Pass the needle through to the back of the work and bring it up by the same pleat, but below the row. Work three stitches again, this time below the row, and repeat to the end. This looks very pretty if you choose either a toning or contrasting thread for the three-stitch groups.

3 Small flowers are easily formed with cable stitch and can be used either to add a dainty spot of colour to a design or to draw together the pleats at the centre of a diamond shape formed by trellis stitch. Work three cable stitches as usual, then take a stitch back over the central two pleats, below the previous stitches, to complete the compact shape of the flower. Fasten off at the back. These flowers must be worked separately, as a long thread carried at the back of the piece might easily catch and would reduce the elasticity of the smocking. A slightly larger double flower may be made by turning the work around from top to bottom after the first three stitches, and working three stitches back again.

4 As with surface honeycomb, this stitch is often stacked in blocks to form shapes and motifs, but cable stitches are set closer together and therefore create a more solid shape. Shapes that are almost rounded may be formed by increasing and decreasing the number of stitches, as seen here with the cat or the tree. This widens the scope for depicting flowers, baskets, trees, animals, people and toys. Start and finish each block separately, turning the work between rows as already described. The stitches may, as can be seen here, be stacked singly or doubled. The blocks will restrict the elasticity of the smocking to some extent, so they should be used sparingly in a design.

Stitch combinations

Having explored the ways in which individual stitches can be varied, the real fun starts when you begin to consider how they may be combined in an apparently infinite number of ways in order to create even more variations.

The chart shown here suggests just a few ideas that you may find interesting, and it is worth making samplers of these and any other variations and combinations of stitches that you may work out for yourself. Samplers are invaluable as reference when you are working out designs, and all your experiments should be kept as a personal checklist.

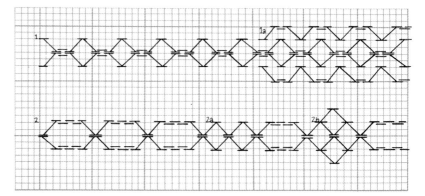

1 **The top and bottom of diamond stitch is formed in the same way as cable, and these two stitches combine together very successfully. If you make three cable stitches instead of one at the bottom of a row of diamond stitch, you will find that small flowers are formed when a second row of diamond stitch is worked, this time with the three cable stitches at the top. This makes a very dainty design for a child's dress, and the pattern may be further extended by adding similar rows above and below the design.**

2 **Try using more cable stitches between the top of the diamond stitches in the first row and the bottom in the second row, elongating the shapes formed between the rows. You may decide to use one or more diamond stitches between the cables in order to change the pattern again, or to add a single diamond above or below the simple diamonds.**

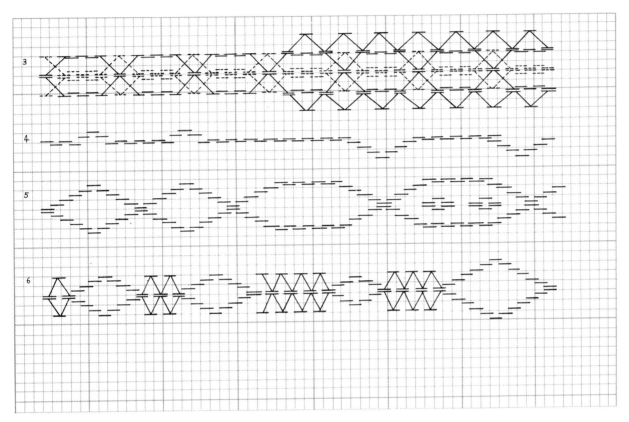

3 The diamond stitch variations given previously demonstrate how rows of diamond stitch can be overlapped, and this chart shows how cable and diamond stitch can be combined in the same way. Very pleasing results are achieved when you use contrasting threads. If you add a single row of diamond stitch above and below the pattern, you can extend it still further.

4 Combinations of cable and wave stitch create some interesting variations: just three steps of wave stitch, spaced at intervals along a line of cable, will break the rigidity of the line and may perhaps be used to echo the peak of a diamond shape in the next row of stitching.

5 The diamond shapes formed by wave and trellis may be elongated by using cable stitches. This pattern may be further enhanced by cable roses, stitched separately at the centre of the enclosed space.

6 Try combining surface honeycomb and wave stitch in the same line, altering the spacing to achieve a pleasing effect.

Embroidery stitches

Surface embroidery stitches can be used to add further embellishments to a smocking design. French knots and bullion knots make tiny flowers which, like cable stitch flowers, form effective central points inside diamond shapes. Alternatively, you may choose to scatter them across a design, or even continue them at random outside the smocked area.

Bullion knots can be used singly to draw pleats together, or you can form them into attractive rose motifs by placing two knots horizontally, one above the other, then coiling three more knots around the first pair. You might choose to complete the image by scattering chain stitch leaves around the roses.

Satin stitch, worked across two or more pleats, forms a solid block of colour and can be used to give body to a light-weight pattern. Satin stitch blocks may also be added to smocked motifs; to make the trunk of a tree, for example.

Beads may be incorporated into smocking to add to the richness of the stitchery: thread a small bead on your needle after the first stage of honeycomb stitch, then continue with the second stage, so that the bead is held firmly and lies on top of the pleat.

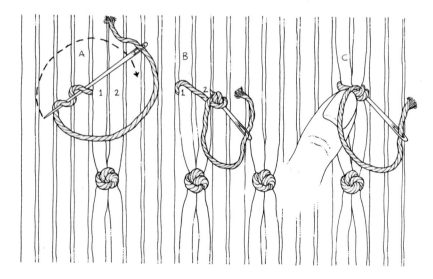

1 To draw two pleats together with a french knot, bring the thread out to the left-hand side of a pleat at point 1, then wrap the thread around the needle two or three times (A). Twist the needle and bring the point back into the right-hand side of the second pleat at point 2 (B). Push the twisted thread down the needle to form a knot. Hold this against the fabric with your left thumb while you pull the needle and thread gently through the knot and out at the back of the work, and fasten off with two back stitches. When knots are spaced apart, each must be started and finished separately.

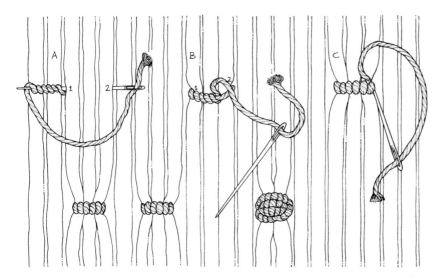

2 To make a bullion knot, bring the needle out at the left-hand side of a pleat at point 1. Backstitch through 2, 3 or 4 pleats as required at point 2. Bring the needle out at point 1 again, but do not pull right through. Twist the thread around the needle 6 or 7 times, depending on the width of the stitch (A). Hold the twists in place with your left thumb, and gently pull the needle and thread out through the twists (B). Make sure the twists are lying evenly along the thread and tighten the knot by pulling the thread. Pass the needle through to the back of the work at point 2 (C).

3 For satin stitch, bring the needle out at the left-hand side of a pleat at point 1. Take a back stitch horizontally across two, three or four pleats into point 2, bringing the needle out just below point 1 (A). Continue taking stitches across the pleats until you have made a satin stitch block of the required size (B).

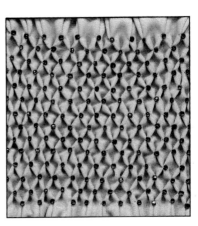

Honeycomb stitch has here been worked on a satin fabric and embellished with beading. The sample might be used to decorate the flap of an evening bag.

Balancing the design

Before starting on a piece of smocking intended for a practical purpose, you will also need to work out how the design will fit into the number of pleats formed when you gather up the width of fabric. It is important that any motif or peak of a geometric shape should be centred, and the main shapes spread evenly across the width, so that the pattern is exactly balanced. The design on the little red dress on page 37, for example, has the three basket motifs spaced evenly apart, and the large zigzag shapes formed by wave stitch finish at the same point at either end of the smocking. A balanced effect like this can be worked out on graph paper by counting the number of pleats taken up by each shape and relating this to the pleats in the fabric.

To make sure that the design is centred on the fabric, mark the centre pleat after gathering is complete by basting down the length of the pleat with brightly coloured thread.

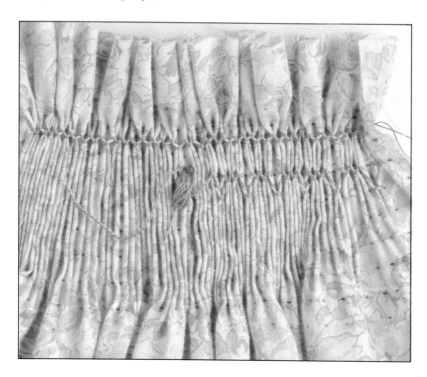

Right The three basket motifs on the dress are formed by stacked double cable, with satin-stitch flowers set against a background of diamond stitch and edged with rows of cable stitch. Above and below this panel, wave and trellis stitch shapes are decorated with cable-stitch flowers. The colours of the smocking are repeated in the collar, which has a faggot-stitched binding.

Left When stitching a centred design, take enough embroidery thread for the whole row. Working from the centre of the design, start smocking from the central pleat towards the right-hand side: pull the thread only halfway through at the first stitch; pin the long end to the fabric, and complete the smocking out to one side only, using the remaining thread. Turn the work around from top to bottom; unpin the long end and thread it through the needle, then smock from the centre to the opposite edge, repeating the pattern exactly. In this way, you can avoid making a joint at the centre point. The balance of the pattern will now be established, and the rest of the pattern can be started at the edge in the normal way.

Reverse smocking

This technique is used to control the pleats on the wrong side of the fabric in areas where there is no surface smocking. This could be at the centre of a large trellis pattern, where the pleats are not covered by stitching and would stretch out of shape unless held in place at the back. When a space that is wider than usual is required between the rows of a design, the use of reverse smocking is advisable. It can also be used to create a free area on the surface of the pleats where you wish to stitch a motif or to add free surface embroidery. If the pleats are controlled at the back of the fabric in this way, the front surface becomes rippled and slightly distorted when the gathering threads are removed, and this can introduce an interesting texture to contrast with the stitchery.

The effect varies from stitch to stitch: look at the back of the stitch samples you have made; stretch them out gently, and see how the pleats become slightly twisted out of line. In this way, you can judge which stitch is the most suitable to use for reverse stitching in order to give you the effect that you want on the front. Cable and outline stitch control the pleats firmly and result in a faint line showing across the surface. More open stitches, such as surface honeycomb and diamond stitch, will give a lighter effect and are more elastic. Honeycomb stitch should not be used for reverse smocking, as the threads that run behind the pleats will be seen on the right side. Whichever stitch is used, only a small amount of fabric should be picked up, otherwise the backs of the stitches may show on the right side.

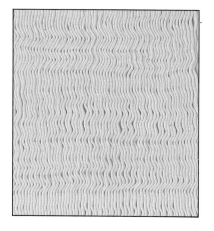

Reverse smocking can be used to distort the fabric into attractive rippled patterns.

North American smocking

This is really a method of fabric manipulation, and is not elastic like English smocking. The fabric is marked with a grid, and is then pulled into shapes with the stitches. The technique should be worked on a firm fabric that will not flatten or crush, so that the shape of the pattern is maintained.

The lattice pattern (1, 2) creates a woven effect, and was once very popular for decorating velvet cushions. It now has a more varied application for cuffs and waistbands on dresses, blouses and lightweight suits. Regular check fabric, such as gingham, is ideal for this

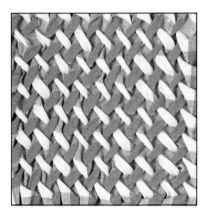

A lattice pattern is here worked on gingham, so that the white and brown squares appear to cross over one another.

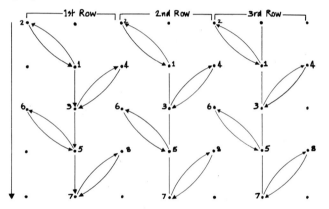

1 Using strong thread, with a knot at one end, pick up a small dot of fabric at dot 1. Pick up dot 2 and pull the fabric down to dot 1, then stitch the two firmly together.

2 Take a backstitch at dot 3, keeping the fabric flat between dots 1/2 and 3. Pick up dot 4 and pull the fabric down to meet dot 3. Stitch them firmly together. Continue in this way down the first row, keeping the fabric flat between the uneven numbers. Work subsequent rows in the same way.

technique, as the squares form the grid pattern and the alternating colours make an interesting pattern. If you are using a plain fabric, mark out the grid on the wrong side with an air- or water-soluble pen, or use a large square dot transfer: the size of the grid will depend on the weight of the fabric. The flower pattern (3, 4) is worked on a grid in a similar way, to create raised shapes like flower heads.

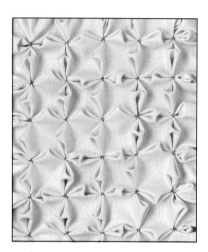

A sample of traditional flower pattern smocking, worked to a square grid, as shown in the diagram.

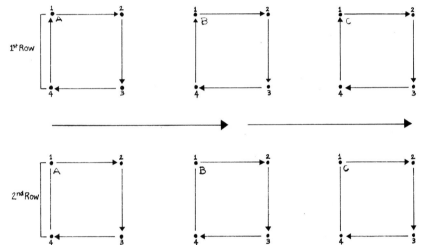

3 For the flower pattern, mark a grid of squares on the right side of the fabric. With strong sewing thread, leave a knot at the back and start at corner 1, box A. Pick up a small piece of fabric at each corner, with small stitches slanting to the centre of the box. Pick up corner 1 again; pull the thread tightly, drawing the corners together, and secure them with a back stitch. Take the thread to the back of the work; bring it out at the corner of box B, and make a back stitch, keeping the fabric flat between A and B. Stitch each box in this and subsequent rows in the same way.

Right *This cushion cover by Jean Hodges is worked in flower pattern, with some of the petals of the flowers pushed back to the wrong side, thus creating a design in which the flowers stand out in contrast against flat areas.*

CHAPTER 3

DESIGNING TRADITIONAL PATTERNS

Tension and texture

If you are new to smocking, and have been following the instructions so far, you will by now have mastered the basic smocking stitches and made some experiments with stitch variations. Already, your smocking will be showing your own individual technique, for no two people work in exactly the same way. Tension and the placement of stitches will always vary from one person to another, even though both may be working correctly.

The next stage is to confirm your individuality and derive great satisfaction from planning your own designs. An infinite number of patterns may be built up by linking different stitches and devising new variations. When you consider that, quite apart from the selection of stitches, the choice of fabric, threads and colours is also a matter of personal taste, it is easy to appreciate that your smocking projects will be unique.

You will also have observed that it is not only the stitches that make patterns, but that the pleats are pulled in different directions by the stitches. They may be pressed side by side or pulled apart to form chevrons. A group of pleats may be pulled together by a cable flower or bullion knot, or fanned out by wave or trellis stitch. The texture and depth formed by this distortion of the pleats is one of the most pleasing characteristics of smocking. The spaces of unstitched pleats make a good counterpoint to the areas of smocking and also contribute to the elasticity of the work. This shows particularly well on many of the old smocks, where the stitches are worked in thread of the same colour as the fabric, so that the texture of the pleats is as important as the stitches.

In this sampler, the stitches are worked in thread of the same colour as the fabric, so that the distortions and patterns of the pleats are clearly seen.

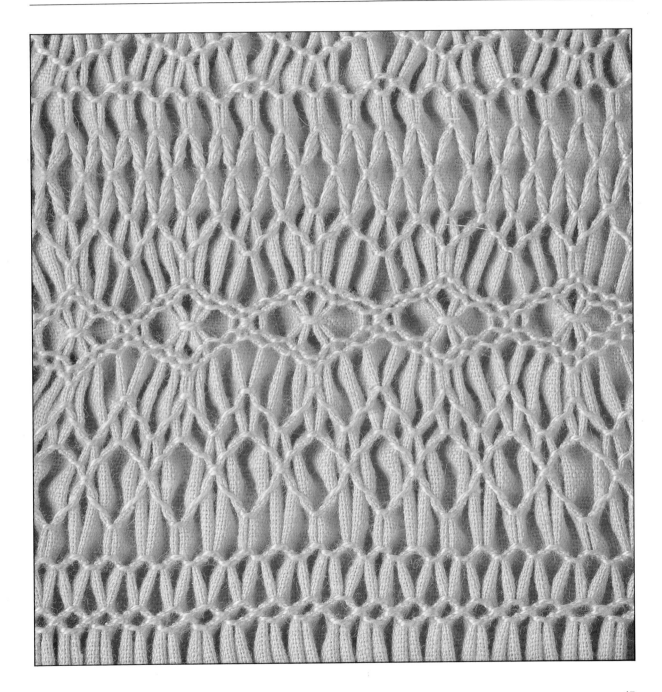

Designing on paper

When you begin to work out a new design, it is best to try out some ideas on paper rather than working directly on fabric: this will enable you to see the overall proportions of the design before you make a sample.

The guidelines that are given here are intended as aids to developing designs, but they are only suggestions. Try these and other ways that may occur to you to build up patterns, thinking of possible stitches all the time. Even absent-minded doodles may suggest ideas to you. Look around for objects that may be used as design sources – the patterns on tiles, carpets or pottery may inspire you. Textile folk arts, in particular, may prove a rich source of inspiration for designs, whether these are found in the borders of eastern rugs and carpets, or in cross-stitch and other embroidery patterns. Even simple patchwork patterns may be suitable for conversion into smocking designs, and may also suggest interesting colour combinations. Cut triangular shapes from cardboard and move them around and over one another to create new shapes. Any geometric shape that can be repeated to form a pattern may be interpreted in stitchery.

When you have created a basic pattern, check that it is balanced, making sure that no area is so concentrated that it makes the design top heavy, or so light that there will not be enough stitchery in that area to control the pleats. Proportion is also important, and it is essential to consider where the smocking will be used. A large design would overwhelm a baby's dress, while a tiny design would be lost on a large item. You also need to decide whether the pattern can be reversed from a centre point, or whether you should have different patterns, from the top row down to the bottom.

The next stage is to work out which stitches will best interpret the shapes that you have chosen: it is here that stitch samplers prove an invaluable reference. When you have chosen your stitches, draw out the design in chart form, as for the sampler already given on page 25. Try out a small sample of the design on a scrap of the chosen fabric, to see how well the stitches work and to help you to decide on a colour scheme.

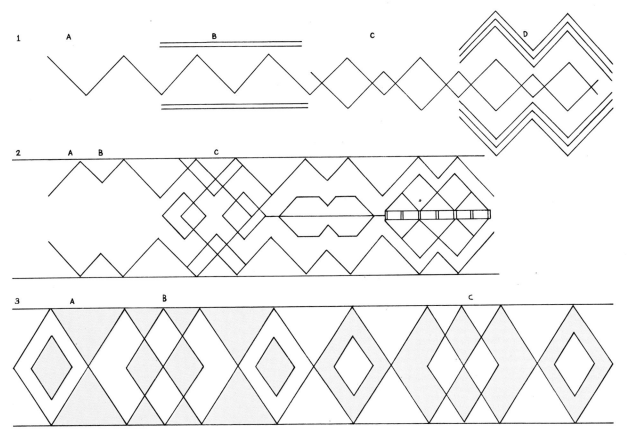

1 Start by drawing a zigzag line across the page. Next, edge the zigzag with straight lines at the top and bottom: these lines could, perhaps, represent a pattern formed from cable stitch and diamond stitch. Alternatively, overlap the first zigzag row with a second: this could be interpreted in trellis and wave stitch. You might add further zigzag lines above and below, echoing the centre lines: these could all be stitched in tones of one colour, using wave stitch.

2 Draw two parallel lines, then draw matching zigzags, making triangles of different sizes along each line. Fill in the spaces between with a variety of shapes. Several stitches could be used to interpret these lines – the choice is up to you.

3 Continuing the theme of diamonds and triangles, draw a pattern with interlocking shapes. Shade in some of the shapes with colour: this will represent the stitches, and the unshaded areas will be left unstitched. Try reversing the shaded and unshaded areas, changing the look of the pattern completely.

Texture and reverse smocking

The rippled texture of reverse smocking can become a feature in its own right and may be used with surface stitchery to simulate a bib front or yoke on a child's dress, or create a pattern for a cushion front. When reverse and surface stitching are used together, you will see that the section of pleats stitched by reverse smocking appear to protrude forward, whereas the pleats that are surface smocked seem to recede. This difference between the two types of smocking can be further enhanced by adding embroidered flowers or bullion knots at the point of change from one to the other.

Right The bodice of this striped dress by Rose Glennie is smocked from shoulder to waist, with reverse smocking used in contrast with surface stitchery to simulate a bib front, emphasized by an edging of embroidered flowers.

Below The body of the fish, formed with surface honeycomb and beading, appears to recede into the background of reverse smocking.

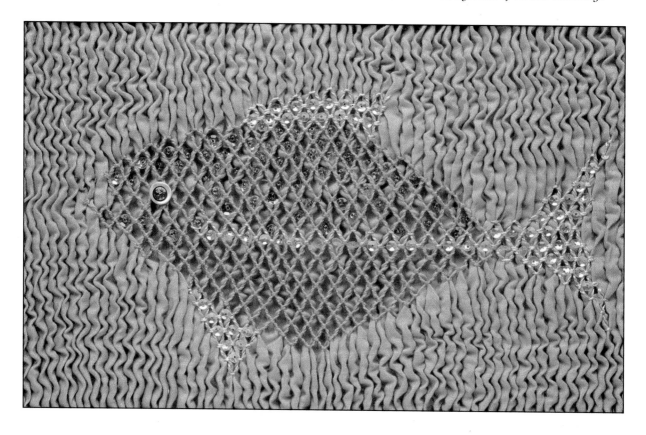

Patterned fabric and colour

All the samples so far have been made with plain fabrics so that the stitches can be clearly seen. However, patterned fabrics lend themselves equally well to smocking, presenting scope for more subtle colour combinations. The choice of coloured threads must be considered carefully, as any decoration on a patterned background can merge into the pattern and almost disappear if the colour of the threads is not strong enough.

It is natural to hold a skein of embroidery thread over the fabric and match the colours exactly. It is worth remembering, however, that a smocked garment will usually be seen at a distance, and the colours of the patterned fabric will merge. Hold the fabric at arm's length and look at it with your eyes half closed, to see which colours predominate. Also, a single length of embroidery thread will appear much paler than the whole skein, so take a length out and try the

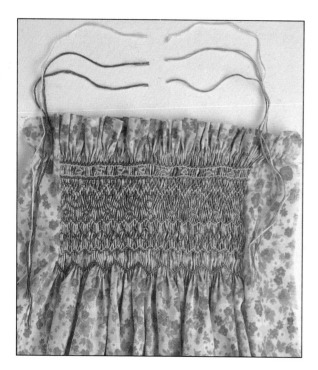

Left *Threads that are exactly matched to the fabric appear to merge into it, whereas threads in stronger colours show up more clearly.*

Right *A large motif is squeezed into a narrow shape when gathered.*

Far right *The small flowers of the printed design are here merged together by the gathers.*

colour again: you will almost certainly find that you need to use a brighter, stronger colour than you first thought, if the stitches are to show well against the background. This does not mean that the colours should be harsh and unsympathetic to the fabric. When the smocking is complete, it should appear as an integral part of the patterned fabric rather than just added to it.

When a patterned fabric is gathered ready for smocking, the pleats will distort the pattern, presenting an almost abstract surface for the stitchery. A large motif will be squeezed into a narrow, fragmented shape, and a small design will be scattered and submerged by the gathers. These effects add further interest to the final result. Transfer dots may not show up sufficiently well on patterned fabric, especially small floral designs, so you will have to use the tissue paper method of gathering. It is always worth trying out a small sampler to experiment with the colours and stitches. Stand back from the sampler to gauge the effect from a short distance.

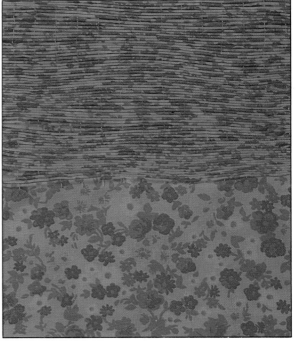

Checks

A fabric with a regular, repetitive pattern needs no preparation with smocking dots, as the pattern can be used as a guide for the gathering threads. Woven gingham is often used as a base for smocking, because the squares are an excellent guide for both gathering and stitching, making this a popular choice of fabric for beginners.

Gingham is usually woven in one colour, with white as a contrast, so that the resulting fabric has squares of plain colour and white, plus squares of the two combined. It is possible to choose which colour you wish to emphasize by placing the gathering stitches in a certain way: for example, if you pick up the centre of each coloured square on the wrong side and pull up the gathering threads, then just the white squares and the combination squares will show on the right side. Conversely, if the centre of each white square is picked up with the gathering thread, a much darker effect is created on the right side. When the corners of every square are picked up, all the colours will show on the right side.

Try various ways of gathering to see the effects. You will notice that each method creates pleats of a different size, and you will need to take this into consideration when estimating the width of material required. Gingham is available in patterns of different sizes – 6mm (¼in.) squares are probably the most useful. You will not be able to create the dramatic contrasting effects just described with gingham that has large squares, as the pleats would be too deep, just as tiny squares would form very small pleats. However, gingham with squares of 3mm (⅛in.) or up to 2cm (¾in.) may be used, and you will find that it is possible to achieve a wide range of effects, depending on whether you gather over several small squares or pick up two or three times in a large square.

Any printed check fabric can be gathered and smocked in the same way as gingham, but you will have to make sure that the printing is true to the grain of the fabric or the pleats may not hang properly. This will not matter if you are making the smocking to be cut and inserted into a garment, however. In the case of gingham, of course, the checked pattern is woven and therefore runs with the grainlines of the fabric.

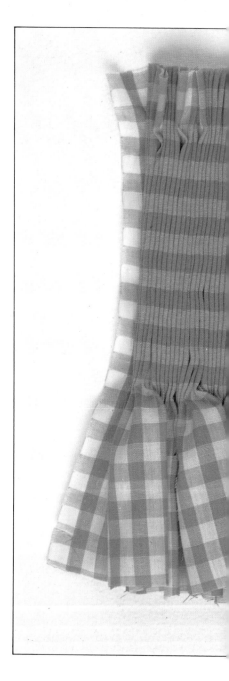

Smocking gathers may be used to emphasize either the dark or the light squares of a checked design: on the left, the centre of each white square has been picked up by the gathering threads, on the right, the coloured squares have been picked up.

Stripes

Fabric that is woven or printed with stripes in two colours and of regular width is often worth considering for smocking, as the stripes may be used as a guide for gathering. As with checks, you can dictate the shading of the pleats: if you pick up a light stripe with the gathering thread on the wrong side, the dark stripe will appear on the right side of the fabric, and vice versa.

To obtain a straight line of gathers, draw guide lines with a water- or air-soluble pen across the wrong side of the fabric, at right angles to the stripes and an even distance apart.

Another idea for using stripes is to turn the fabric and gather horizontally along the stripes. This may form an interesting contrast, with the folds of the pleats running at right angles to the stripes. If you then match the colour of the embroidery thread to one of the stripes, and work stitches only over the depth of the stripe of the other colour, an impression of insertion stitchery can be given. When this idea is used for a garment, an even-weave fabric is needed, for the cloth to hang properly.

If you gather a fabric with stripes of uneven width, you can create blocks of colour, and these may be further emphasized with stitchery.

Try out ideas with a range of fabrics, playing with different gathers and colours. Keep small samples of any experiments which you make, as these may inspire ideas for future projects. Remember, however, that you will have to be able to buy the identical fabric in order to reproduce an idea exactly: the sample will only give a general impression of the effect you may achieve, but an unusual width of stripe may not be easy to find a second time.

As with checked fabrics, it makes a great deal of difference whether the design is printed or woven into the fabric. In the case of printed designs, it is quite possible that the stripes do not run absolutely true to the grain of the fabric, in which case the pleats will not hang evenly. In the latter case, the pattern, being created as the fabric is woven, must run along the grainlines. It is therefore best to make sure which type of fabric you have before smocking, unless you intend to cut and inset the finished smocking (see pages 64–5).

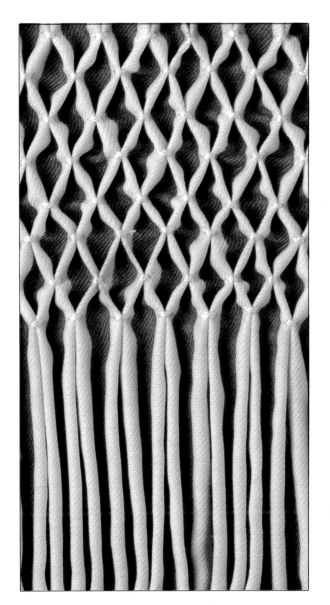 

These two samples show the same pattern stitched on the same blue and white striped fabric. In the sample on the left-hand side, the blue stripes have been taken to *the back by the gathering: white stripes have been picked up by the gathering threads to create the sample on the right.*

Colour

As can be seen on traditional smocks and on some of the samples shown here, self-colour smocking places an emphasis on texture and the movement of the pleats, and this remains an important characteristic of smocking. Nowadays, however, more interest is shown in using colour in fabrics and threads, especially for fashion items. This makes us more aware of the stitchery, but colours need to be chosen with care. A chaotic mass of colour should never be allowed to overwhelm and obscure the texture.

Taste in colour is very personal, and everyone has a favourite colour scheme. This is built up over the years and is reflected in the clothes we wear and soft furnishings about the home. You will find that you instinctively put one colour with another and choose colour schemes with which you are familiar, without giving it much thought. This may be fine, as far as it goes, but it is worth spending time thinking about colour and doing some experiments that may open up new possibilities for future projects.

Look carefully at everyday objects around you, and identify the colours in them. Photographs, pictures in magazines and postcards will suggest colour schemes, and are worth collecting. Fabrics, wrapping paper, carpets and tiles may contain colour combinations that you have not thought of before. Inspiration may come from man-made objects ~ in the range of colours in a brick wall; in the lovely bronze tones of rusting metal, or the faded colours of peeling paintwork.

Photographs of natural objects, like this scattering of leaves, can provide highly successful colour combinations for smocking schemes, especially if you take care to analyse and reproduce the same balance of colours.

Devising a colour scheme

Nature provides endless sources of inspiration: choose an object, such as a leaf, stone, shell or fruit. Study it carefully and try to identify the colours contained in it: look at the tones of colour revealed in the highlights and shadows; examine the stems, veins or blemishes, and notice how even the smallest areas may contain a colour that gives just a spot of contrast. Next, consider the proportions of colour, and decide which is the main one and how many subsidiary colours there are.

Now try to match all these colours as closely as possible to threads

A turnip is used here as a source for a colour scheme of cream, sandy yellow and mauve. The chosen threads are wrapped over a card and a collage of fabric scraps is made for future reference.

in your collection. Cut a narrow strip of card and cover it with double-sided adhesive tape. Wrap the card with the threads, using the same proportions as those in your chosen object, and see if this is a colour scheme that you would like to use. Take the same colours again to wrap another piece of card. This time, change the proportions, so that the main colour on the first card is now a subsidiary colour on the second, and you will see how the effect is changed. Matching pieces of fabric or paper can be made into a collage as an alternative to the threads, and all these experiments should be kept for future reference. The card strips are very convenient because you can lay them against a background fabric to get an instant impression of a colour scheme.

Selecting threads

The next step is to translate your colour scheme into a smocking project. Consideration must be given to the type of fabric you are going to use and how it will affect the colour. For instance, a shiny satin or a pile fabric like velvet will catch the light and tend to change colour, depending on which way you look at it, whereas a mat surface, like wool, will stay much the same.

The colour of the threads will change in relation to one another, especially when overlapping stitches are used. The density of colour will depend on the type of stitch. The colour will appear to be much stronger when you are using a stitch in which the threads are close together, such as cable, than when using diamond stitch, which is more open. Threads can appear to change colour against different backgrounds, and shiny threads will catch the light. Although they may be paler in colour, they will as a result show up more clearly than a mat thread.

The proportions of colour are equally important: a very strong colour will make all the others appear faded and will dominate the design unless it is used in small amounts. Equal amounts of each colour can be dull and repetitive, but will be livened up with a touch of a contrast colour.

The importance of trying out a sample before you embark on a new project is obvious: however tempting it may seem to skip this stage, a sample will save time and disappointment. Stand back and look at the sample in the place where you expect the final project to be used; for example, in the room where a picture is to hang or a cushion to be placed. If you are making a garment for a child or an adult, hold a sample against them; and if the design is intended for evening wear, see how it looks in artificial light.

The yellow, gold, tan and green colours of harvest time were the inspiration for the colour scheme chosen for the smocked panel of this cream silk dress, made for a late summer wedding. The detail of the finely smocked panel includes sheaves of wheat embroidered with french knots over a background of diamond stitch.

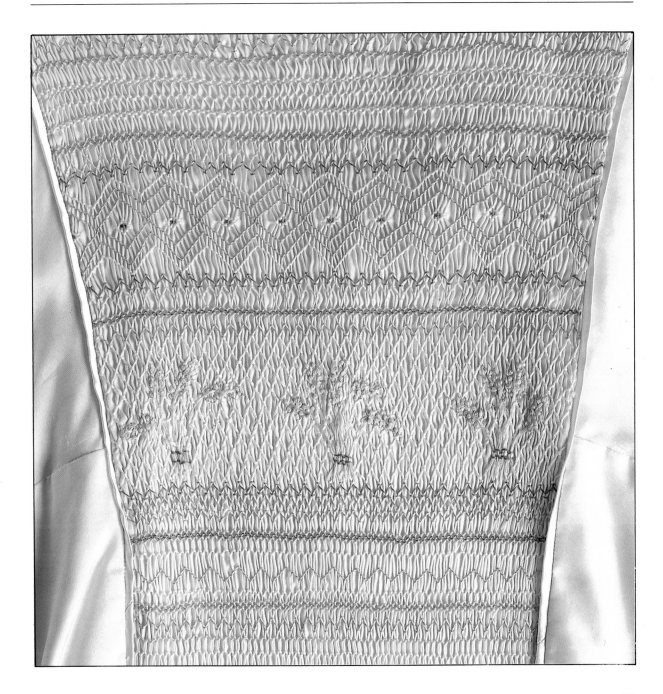

CHAPTER 4

APPLYING SMOCKING

Estimating fabric requirements

Designing smocking patterns is enjoyable and creative, but if you wish to translate a smocking idea into a practical project, the first stage will be to decide how much fabric you will require. Three to four times the finished width is usually given as a general guide to the width of fabric that will be needed for a piece of smocking. This means that 15 or 20cm (6 or 8in.) of fabric will be reduced to 5cm (2in.) of smocking. However, a more accurate estimate will depend on the factors listed below.

The type of fabric

When a thick fabric is gathered, it will form bulky pleats, each of which will take up more space than a pleat of fine fabric, gathered at the same spacing. As a result, a narrower width of thick fabric than of fine will achieve the same width of finished smocking.

The size of pleat

If the smocking dots are widely spaced, for example at intervals of 12mm (½in.), more fabric will be gathered up than if the dots are set at a 3mm (⅛in.) spacing.

The choice of stitch

Some stitches, such as cable and outline, hold the pleats more firmly together and are less elastic than others, such as honeycomb. Concentrated areas of stitching and motifs will also limit the elasticity of the smocking. So the overall design and the individual stitches must also be taken into consideration.

Tension

Everyone works to a different tension, and you will know whether you yourself stitch lightly, so that your smocking stretches easily, or

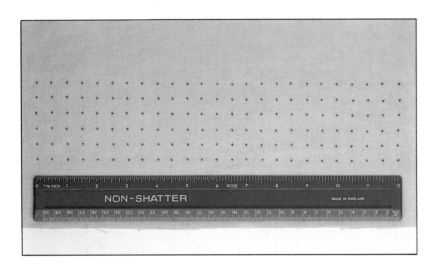

1 Measure the width of your sample fabric and count the number of dots per row before gathering.

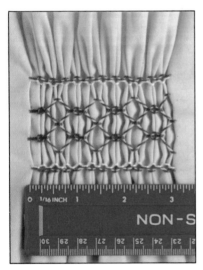

2 Make the smocking, including an example of each of the stitches that you intend to use in your design. Remove the gathering threads and measure the width of your completed sample.

whether your work is difficult to stretch because of tight stitching. Allow more fabric if you stitch to a tight tension, because the finished smocking should fit easily into its place without being stretched excessively.

Making a sample (1, 2)

As you will gather, it is essential that before you embark on a project you make a sample piece, using the fabric, smocking dots, thread and stitches that you intend for the main piece.

Once you have made and measured the sample, as shown, you can then calculate the width of fabric required for the finished piece and the number of dots needed to mark it, in order to allow the finished piece to fit comfortably into its allotted place. For example, if the sample was made with 30cm (12in.) of fabric, using rows of 24 dots, spaced 12mm (½in.) apart, and this was reduced to 7.5cm (3in.) when smocked, then you will need four times the required finished width. If, say, the smocking is to fit into a dress yoke 25cm (10in.) wide, you will need a 100cm (40in.) width of fabric, marked with rows of 80 dots.

The length of fabric required will be governed by the pattern, but it is prudent to allow an extra 12mm (½in.), as smocking entails a slight lengthwise take-up of fabric.

Adapting commercial patterns for children

So few of the available commercial patterns include areas of smocking that it is often necessary to adapt ordinary patterns when you wish to make smocked clothes for children. This is easily done: all you need is a pencil, paper cutting scissors, a long ruler, and a length of pattern paper, such as kitchen shelf paper or wallpaper lining.

First measure the width of finished smocking that will be required. On the first example shown here, the smocking is to run along a dress yoke. When measuring your pattern to find the length of smocking that will be required, it is important to remember to measure the stitching line, not the outer line of the seam allowance, and to exclude seam allowances at either end of the line from your calculations. Make a sample, in order to calculate the extent of shrinkage that will be caused by the smocking.

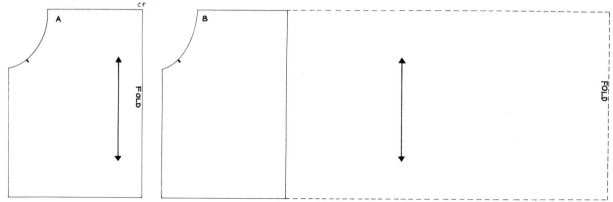

1 To alter a pattern in order to set in smocking at the yoke of a child's dress, lay lining paper on a flat surface and place the commercial bodice pattern piece on it. Draw around the pattern piece, which will usually be half the front section, with the centre front placed to the fold (A). Measure along the stitching line of the *yoke*, to discover the finished length of smocking required. Measure the seamline of the yoke, rather than that of the bodice, as this will probably be designed to be slightly gathered, and your smocking could be too wide if you base your calculations on this measurement.

Assuming the finished smocking length is 25cm (10in.), and the required fabric width is four times this, the pattern piece must be extended to measure 50cm (20in.) along the stitching line on the bodice front (remembering that this is placed to the fold). Measure out along the upper edge, as shown, to the required width. Draw a straight line across, then draw the new centre front, parallel to the old one. Extend the bottom line to meet it. Transfer marks and grainlines from the old pattern and note that the new centre front must also be placed to the fold of the fabric. Cut out the new pattern section; then cut out the rest of the dress, using the commercial pattern (B).

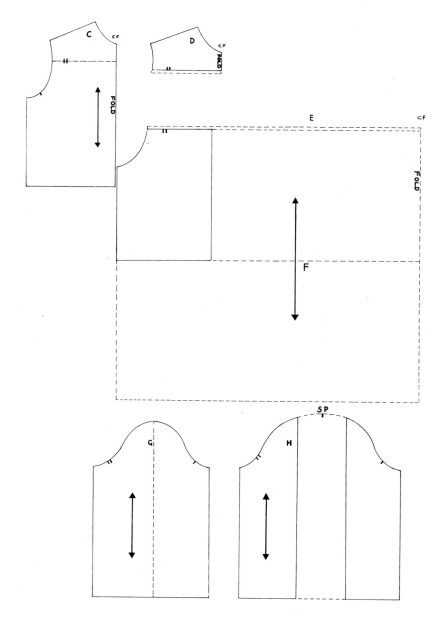

2 A plain bodice front can be divided into a yoke and lower bodice, which can be extended ready for smocking. Draw around the whole bodice section, as before, then mark the lower edge of the new yoke with a straight line across from the armhole to the centre front. Draw a balance mark across this line about 2.5cm (1in.) from the armhole, to show where the two sections will match (C). Trace around the new yoke section, adding the same seam allowance as on the rest of the pattern, plus any other balance marks, grainlines and centre front fold markings (D). Extend the rest of the bodice section, just as before, remembering to transfer markings and to add a seam allowance to the top edge (E). If you wish, this bodice section can be lengthened, as shown, to include a skirt (F).

3 The same method of extension can be applied to a sleeve, if you wish to introduce smocking at the sleeve head and cuff. This time you will need to draw around the whole sleeve pattern, and then cut it down the centre, from top to bottom (G). Pull the two sections apart to the width required, and then redraw the pattern, curving slightly at the sleeve head to produce a smooth line. Transfer balance marks and grainlines and mark the new shoulder point at the centre of the sleeve head (H).

Cutting the smocking

Straight edges can be extended easily. It is more difficult to extend a pattern on which the smocking will run up to the neckline and shoulder. To achieve this, the bodice pattern would have to be cut in several places and pulled apart, distorting the shape. The same

The bodice of the white pinafore was smocked on a straight length of fabric, using colours found in the flowered fabric of the dress. The neckline was then cut and bound, and lace shoulder frills were added.

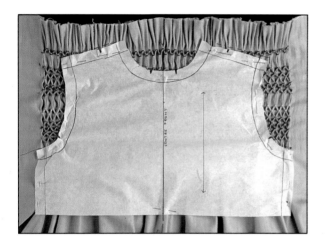

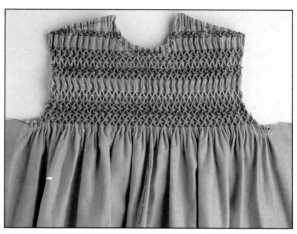

1 If your pattern piece only covers half the bodice, and the centre front is placed on a fold, cut a new pattern to cover the whole area. (This is done by drawing around the cutting lines of the pattern, flipping it over along the foldline, and drawing in the opposite section.) Place the new pattern piece over the smocking, matching the centre front to the central pleat and keeping the pleats in line with the marked grainline. Pin the pattern in place. Baste all around the pattern to mark the cutting line, using a bright, contrasting thread.

2 Remove the pins and the pattern piece, and machine stitch just inside the marked cutting line, using a small stitch that will prevent the smocking stitches from unravelling when they are cut. Finally, cut out the smocked section, following the basted cutting line, and make up the garment in the usual way.

problem would apply if you wished to alter a pattern to allow smocking over a whole sleeve or waistcoat. Even if the pattern were to be adapted successfully, it would be difficult to smock evenly into the curved sections and to maintain the balance of the design. The best way to overcome this problem is to work the area of smocking first and then cut out the shape from the ready-smocked fabric.

Calculate the width of fabric required, allowing for seams and unsmocked areas – under the armholes, for example. Cut the fabric to the correct size. Gather and stitch the smocking, taking care to centre the design. Take out all but the top and bottom gathering threads, then steam press to set the pleats.

Insertions

When the fulness of the gathers falling from the smocking is not to be used as part of the design, then the smocking can be considered purely as a stitched and textured panel, worked as a separate piece and inserted into the garment.

This technique is particularly useful for adding restricted areas of smocking to adult clothes. Here, the fulness of gathers may be too bulky, but a panel may be introduced almost anywhere on the garment where an area of decorative texture would add interest to the design. It may take the form of a strip, running right across the front or back of a blouse or dress, or a small section at either side, just below the shoulder. Smocking may be set into the bib front of dungarees, pinafore or sundress, or you might decide to insert a strip down each side of the button stand of a jacket. Areas of smocking may be used in items other than clothes, and a smocked panel inserted into a cushion or box lid, or an accessory such as a bag or belt would add a unique touch of decoration.

The panel may be shaped, rather than a rectangular strip. You might, for example, choose to insert smocking at a curved shoulder or hip yoke, in which case the piece would be smocked and then cut out, as already described. The inserted panel can be made of the same fabric as the rest of the garment or article, but it is often more interesting and stylish to use a contrasting fabric. When the main fabric is heavily textured, or is bulky and difficult to gather, it may be preferable to select a lighter fabric which, when gathered and smocked, will be comparable in weight to the main fabric. A contrast in colour or texture – shiny fabric against a mat wool, for example, or silk against velvet – would be very effective.

A delightful result may be achieved by setting a plain coloured fabric into a patterned one, and smocking the insertion with colours reflecting those found in the pattern. The panel of smocking can be inserted with the pleats running lengthwise, in the usual manner, or horizontally across the garment. The latter introduces another dimension: the play of light on the pleats runs across rather than down, and the patterns made by the smocking stitches are seen in quite a different way.

Right The colours of the flowers on the dress fabric were chosen to smock a panel of plain cream fabric. The pattern piece of the inserted section was then placed over the smocked panel and the outline was stitched. The neck shape was cut, and the panel was inserted into the bodice with pink piping. The collar and cuffs are of plain cream fabric, piped and embroidered.

Below A straight smocked panel, with elephants formed by stacked stitches, has been inserted into the bib front of these dungarees, designed by Sue Wood.

Adapting for insertions

Even more than in the case of children's clothes, there are very few adult patterns that include smocked insertions, but once again, it is very easy to adapt a commercial pattern. All that is necessary is to divide the existing pattern pieces, as shown here, remembering always to add seam allowances to both sides of the dividing line.

If you are in any doubt as to whether a garment will look attractive with the pattern adapted to include a smocked area, trace over the drawing on the front of the packet and colour the outline with your chosen fabric shades, sketching in the smocking that you have devised. This will give you some idea of the finished appearance. Check that the smocking will be seen to its best advantage, and will not be hidden by your arms or the edge of a collar, for example, and that it will fit in naturally with the overall lines of whatever you are making.

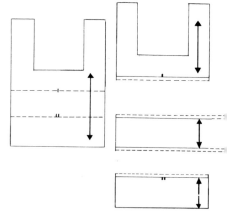

1 Place the pattern piece – in this case, a bib front – on lining paper and pencil around it. Draw in the shape of the panel and add balance marks at the centre, to show where the inserted section aligns with the main garment. Extend the central section to the required width, calculating this as shown, to allow for the smocking. Cut out the new pattern piece, transferring balance marks and straight grainline. Remember to add seam allowances to both sides of the new piece, and to the cut edges of the remaining sections of the existing pattern.

Fine white cotton was chosen for this negligée, by Jean Hodges, which has straight smocked panels, embroidered with bullion knot roses. The panels are edged with narrow binding and joined to the bodice with faggot stitching, to create an openwork seam. Tiny tucks and feather stitching decorate the bodice, sleeves and hem.

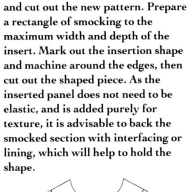

2 The same method is used to make a new pattern of panels to be inserted at each side of a button stand. The pair of smocked sections will be cut with the grain running across the panel, so mark the new pattern piece accordingly. When inserted, the horizontally lying pleats will show the stitching patterns in quite a different way.

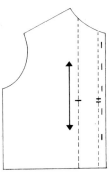

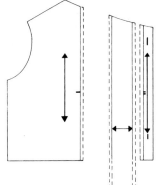

3 In the previous two examples, the fabric is cut out, using the new pattern, and is then smocked, ready for insertion. If you are adapting a pattern to include a shaped section, it is better to cut ready-prepared smocking. Draw the shaped area on the original pattern piece, but do not extend it like the strips shown in the previous steps. Add balance marks, straight grainlines and new seam allowances, and cut out the new pattern. Prepare a rectangle of smocking to the maximum width and depth of the insert. Mark out the insertion shape and machine around the edges, then cut out the shaped piece. As the inserted panel does not need to be elastic, and is added purely for texture, it is advisable to back the smocked section with interfacing or lining, which will help to hold the shape.

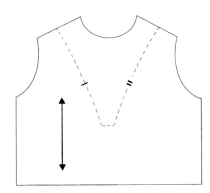

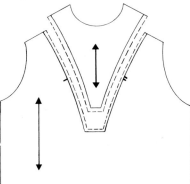

Curved smocking

Smocking can be cut to shape, as has been shown, but in this case the pleats and stitching patterns will remain vertical or horizontal, whatever the shape of the insertion. It is, however, possible to curve the smocking itself, so that the pleats and stitching echo the shape of the seamline. If you are edging a shallow neckline or putting smocking around a crescent-shaped bag or cushion, a straight strip of smocking may be gently manipulated into a shallow curve, provided the stitches at the outside edge of the curve are sufficiently elastic.

If the curve is a deep one, it is not so easy to use a straight strip of smocking: the pleats at the inside edge will be packed tightly together, while the fabric will be stretched almost flat at the outer edge. While it may be acceptable for a bag or cushion, a straight strip curved to fit a high neckline would tend to produce too much bulk at the neck. This bulk is difficult to control neatly unless a very fine fabric is used. A simple technique for coping with the problem is to widen the sheet of smocking dots to accommodate the curve, as shown.

If the pattern for a curved neckline also includes raglan sleeves, then the bodice-to-sleeve seams should be stitched and trimmed before smocking. When you are spreading out the dots, make sure that a line of dots runs down each seamline, so that these points are picked up with the gathering and covered on the right side by the smocking stitches.

Stitches for a curved area must be carefully chosen. The closer, firmer stitches, like outline and cable, should be used on the inside edge of the curve to control the pleats. More open stitches, such as diamond and trellis, should be used in the centre of the design, and the most elastic stitches, like large wave, surface honeycomb and vandyke, at the outside edge of the curve. Even these may have to be 'stepped', exaggerating their natural line, to allow sufficient stretch. The whole curve will become distorted and will not lie flat, if the outside stitches are too tight.

The smocking is often taken into points at the outside edge of a curved shape, allowing greater elasticity. The position of the points

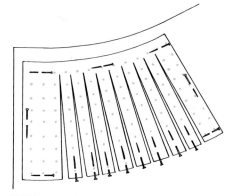

1 To widen smocking dots to accommodate a curve, cut the sheet vertically between rows of dots, cutting from one edge almost to the opposite side. Pin the uncut edge to match the inside edge of the curve on the fabric, then spread the cut sections evenly, fitting them to the shape. Pin them in place and iron them to the fabric in the usual way. The tissue-paper method of marking can be used in the same manner.

The round neckline of this silk crêpe de chine blouse is smocked in toning colours, using cable stitch at the neck, diamond and surface honeycomb for the middle area, and finely stepped surface honeycomb, forming small points, at the outside edge.

2 To take smocking into points, start by making a small sample point, to see how many dots will be needed and to space the points evenly around the design. The dots should be reduced in pairs, one less at each side, until you have a row of three dots at the extreme end, to produce two pleats on the right side. When you have decided how many points you will need, and how deep they will be, trim a sheet of dots into points and, if they are to fit around a curve, slash the rows and spread them out, as already shown.

must be worked out carefully, and sections of the smocking dots must be cut out before pressing, so that the unsmocked area between the points will be unmarked.

When the fabric has been marked, the triangular sections are gathered and pulled up separately, with the threads tied in pairs. Smock down to each point, turning the work at the end of each row. The thread can be taken down behind a pleat and brought up in the correct position to start the next row.

Pointed ends of this type also look very effective when set at the lower edge of a design with a straight upper edge – for example, a waistband or a straight-cut yoke – so that the fabric springs out between the points, allowing the fulness to run down into the skirt or bodice.

Minor adaptations

A major problem when adapting adult patterns is the danger of creating excess bulk. The method described here avoids this by adding small areas of smocking to a commercial pattern. By cutting the pattern and redrawing it to incorporate what amounts to a dart of extra fabric, narrowing to nothing at the unsmocked end of the pattern piece, it is possible to reduce bulk considerably.

Unfortunately, this method of adaptation can only be used for small areas of smocking. If you want to put in a wider piece of smocking, then the method shown for adapting children's clothes must be used, and you will have to try to reduce the amount of excess fabric by making small pleats.

As always, it is important to take note of the direction of the straight grain. In the case of the bodice, the straight grain must run

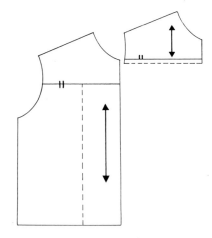

1 Here, a front bodice is divided to create a yoke, with an area of smocking below it. Draw a line from the armhole edge to the centre front, to show the position of the yoke. Add balance marks about 5cm (2in.) in from the armhole, to show where the two sections will meet, and make sure the straight grain is marked on both sections. Cut along the dividing line, then draw around the yoke section on lining paper, adding a seam allowance at the dividing line and transferring all marks.

The sleeve heads of this crêpe de chine blouse were adapted as shown in the diagrams and smocked with cream threads, to match the piping on the collar and cuffs. As a finishing touch, the buttons are embroidered with tiny cream flowers.

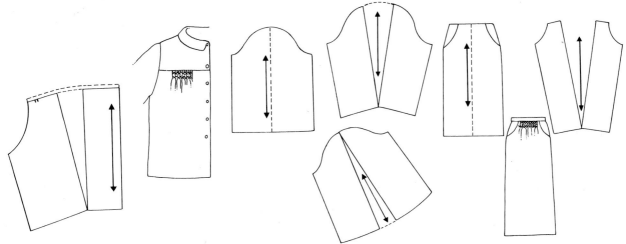

2 On the bodice section, draw and cut down a straight line from the top (yoke) edge, almost to the lower edge. Spread the pieces apart at the top until you have a gap wide enough to allow sufficient extra fabric for a small width of smocking. Redraw the bodice pattern, adding balance marks and a seam allowance at the top edge, and marking in the straight grain. The top and bottom edges will now be slightly curved.

3 The same basic method shown for the bodice can be used to add smocking either at the head or cuff of a sleeve, though in this case the straight grain runs down the centre of the new pattern section.

4 A small section of smocking may also be used to drape gathers at the centre of a straight skirt, again with the straight grain running down the centre of the new pattern piece. Remember, when making an addition of this type, that the finished seamline, including the smocking, must be the same length as on the original pattern, so the smocking must extend a little beyond the new section at each side.

down the centre front. As a result, the more the two sections of the bodice are spread apart, the more the grainlines of the rest will run out of true. It is therefore important, not only to keep the smocked area small, but to use small pleats and keep the rows of gathering threads close together, so that any distortion is kept under control. In the sleeve and skirt adaptations, the straight grain runs down the centre of the addition, but the restrictions remain the same.

When you have adapted the pattern, and before you cut your chosen material, cut the pattern out of an old sheet. Baste the pieces together and try on the sheeting model, so that you can make minor adjustments and ensure that you have achieved the desired effect.

Attaching smocking (1, 2)

If a piece of smocking is to be attached at the top, allowing the rest to fall freely, first complete the stitching, then remove all the gathering threads except the top one, which lies above the first row of stitching. If the piece is to be inserted, leave in both the top and bottom gathering threads.

Cut out the section of the garment – the yoke, for example, or the waistband – to which the smocking is to be attached. Place the smocked piece over this section, with right sides and raw edges together, and match the ends and centre points. Spread the pleats

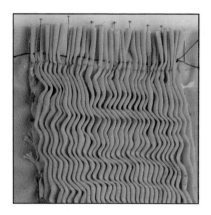

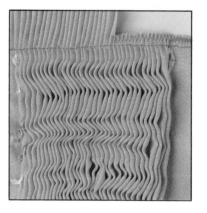

1 When attaching smocking, the stitching line should run between the gathering thread and the first row of smocking. Baste along the stitching line, making small stitches, to hold the pleats firmly. These basting stitches may be left in after machining, so use a matching thread.

2 With the gathered side up, machine along the stitching line. Neaten and trim the raw edges and press away from the smocking. If you prefer, you can attach the smocking by hand.

3 To make piping, fold the piping fabric so that the straight cut edge matches the selvedge. Press the fabric, then open it out and cut along the foldline. Cut a bias strip, following this diagonal and making the strip about 2.5cm (1in.) wide for flat piping, or wide enough to cover the cord and leave 12mm (½in.) for seam allowances for corded piping.

evenly and hold them in place at regular intervals with pins, set at right angles to the edge. Baste and stitch, as shown.

Piping (3, 4, 5, 6)

A narrow strip of piping, whether flat or corded, can be inserted between smocking and the plain fabric, to add a professional finishing touch to a garment or an item of soft furnishing. The colour of the piping may be matched to one of the colours in the smocking, or you might select a matching shiny fabric to contrast with a mat one. In general, most garment piping is flat, and if cording is used it should be fine. Soft furnishing pipings are usually corded.

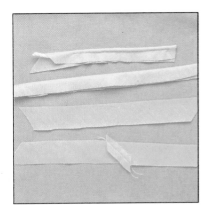
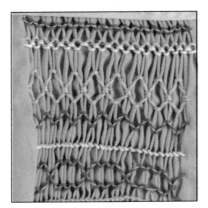
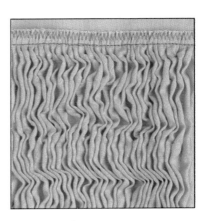

4 Cut along the fold and continue to cut strips of the same width, joining them if necessary to make the desired length. For flat piping, press the bias strip in half lengthwise, with wrong sides together. For corded piping, wrap the bias strip, right side outside, around the cord, and stitch by hand or machine, close to the cord.

5 Place the piping on the right side of the smocking, having first made sure that the smocking is the correct width. The raw edges of the piping should lie 6mm beyond the stitching line of the smocking. Spread the smocking pleats evenly, and pin and baste the piping in position, using small stitches and matching thread.

6 Place the smocked piece over the plain fabric, with right sides together and raw edges and centre points matching. Baste in position, then machine through all layers, with the gathered side up, using the basting line as a guide. Neaten and trim the raw edges and press the seam allowances away from the smocking.

Designs for children

Many women have fond memories of wearing classic party dresses, smocked from yoke to waist and tied with a sash. It would be sad if the children of today were to have no such memories. The casual informal clothes they wear are practical for a busy lifestyle, and the rapidly changing fashions mean that clothes are discarded after being worn a few times.

There is still a place, however, for beautiful, hand-embroidered clothes, to teach the young to appreciate fine workmanship. It is vital that those of us with the enthusiasm to give time to these skills and who enjoy the relaxation and creativity of smocking, should apply our skills in such a way as to appeal to both children and teenagers, and encourage them to learn the craft for themselves.

The elastic characteristic of smocking, however, makes it most practical for the everyday clothes of growing active children, and it can successfully be used for waistbands, yokes and sleeves on dungarees or overalls, shorts, pinafores, dresses and skirts. Inserted areas of smocking on pockets, yokes, cuffs and belts will do much to liven up plain clothes. Try highlighting outerwear, such as jackets, coats and trousers, with areas of smocking, and for these items, think of using it on a larger scale, with brightly coloured, thicker threads to add impact.

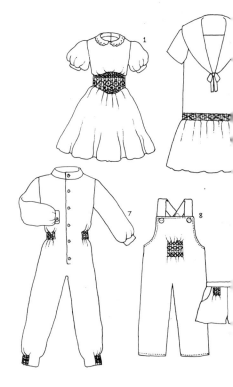

1 Smocking can look charming at the waistband of a skirt or dress, though you must be careful, even with children's clothes, to avoid adding too much bulk.

2 A dropped waistband is perennially stylish and attractive for a young girl, allowing a straight bodice, but plenty of freedom in the skirt.

3 Shoulder bands may be smocked, leaving a narrow frill at the neckline.

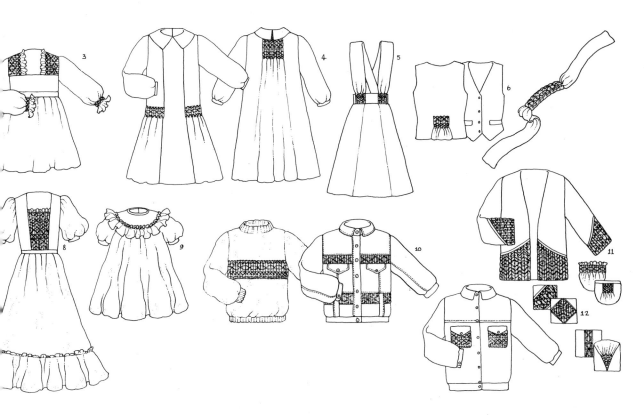

4 A smocked panel below the neck at the back of a dress can be repeated just below the pockets at the front.

5 An adaptation of the pinafore dress has smocking set into the waistband of a skirt, with the gathers running up into wide shoulder straps.

6 A small area of smocking may be used to draw in the back of a waistcoat or make the front of a detached sash.

7 Smocking, perhaps using thicker threads than usual and stitched in bold colours, is an ideal way of gathering the waist band, cuffs and ankles of everyday clothing, such as this all-in-one suit, or of adding a touch of interest to plain shorts or overalls.

8 Smocked insertions are always worth considering as a way of adding interest to a plain front, whether on party clothes or play wear.

9 Smocked ruffles may be used to edge a square or round yoke on a dress, or the back yoke of a jacket.

10 Panels may be inset across a sweater, yoke or jacket, using cut and inserted smocking to avoid an excess width of fabric.

11 Smocked cuffs and pockets transform a plain jacket into best wear.

12 It takes very little time to smock a pocket, creating the detail and fashion interest that children appreciate just as much as adults.

Designs for adults

Smocking lends itself particularly well to evening wear and lingerie, offering a way of creating elegantly draped designs, but it can also be used to lift everyday clothes out of the ordinary. Whatever the current fashion – whether it is for long full skirts or a short, straight look – smocking can be incorporated. If fulness is not desirable, then cut insertions provide the answer. The skill is to pick the fabrics and colours that are either classic and dateless, or up-to-the-minute: subtle texture rather than stitchery may be the look that you should aim for; or maybe you might like to try something highly experimental and modern, perhaps with specially dyed fabrics and threads. The choice is yours, and all that matters is to give your imagination free rein.

1 Smocking lends itself particularly well to decorating draped designs on skirts, cowl necklines and shoulder drapes. For evening wear, try using lurex or metallic threads for the smocking – beads will add further richness to the design. Wool or cotton jersey gather and drape well, and small touches of smocking with shiny threads will lift the dullness of a plain wool dress. Remember to keep fulness on the bodice to a minimum.

2 Smocking, used at an elastic waistline, works as well on a sheer nightdress as on sports wear.

3 Smocked hip panels introduce fulness to a skirt while allowing it to fit snugly to the figure. A touch of smocking, under hip yokes or pockets, will add fulness below hip level and keep the waist-to-hip area smooth and flat. Tiers or ruffles at the base of a skirt are an unusual addition to a design.

4 Sections may be inserted into shoulder and hip yokes, necklines, waistbands and cuffs and pockets. These sections are worked separately, cut into shape, and then inserted so that the pleats run either vertically or horizontally.

5 Smocking can give added interest to the back of a design. It is equally effective for lingerie or evening wear, made from fine fabrics and with dainty stitch patterns, as for jackets and coats in much heavier fabrics, using stitches on a larger scale.

6 You may restrict your smocking to very narrow bands, inserted into the front of a blouse to frame the button placket, or running down the length of a dress or skirt with the fulness released at the base. This can have the same impact as a much larger area of smocking.

7 Consider using the textured fabric made by smocking for the whole of a jacket, perhaps using large-scale honeycomb stitches, and edging the jacket with a quilted band. A fine sheer fabric, smocked and used for the entire bodice of a blouse will make a lovely contrast to the sheer sleeves gathered into matching cuffs. An evening jacket made of silk, with the sleeves covered in smocking, using metallic threads, can be utterly beautiful. In all these cases, the fabric must be smocked first and then cut out, using the appropriate pattern piece.

8 Sleeves offer great scope for decorative smocking. The fulness of fabric from smocking at the sleeve head or from a shoulder yoke, cut in one with the sleeve, falls right down the length of the sleeve, making it hang softly and enhancing the overall design. If you are using heavier fabric, the smocking can be added in the form of inserted bands, framing the sleeve head. Many of the other designs are best stitched with fine fabrics. These will show your smocking to advantage, inspiring the creation of stunning evening wear or enchanting wedding dresses.

Fashion accessories

Smocking is so versatile that not only is the embroidery a charming addition to all types of clothes, but it is equally successful for the decoration of fashion accessories. As accessories account for only a small proportion of the overall outfit, they lend themselves particularly well to experimentation with a range of unusual fabrics and threads and to additional decoration with beads and ribbons, which would perhaps be overwhelming when used on the main garment.

Belts (1, 2, 3)

The elastic quality of smocking makes it ideal for belts, which can be made as shown. Reverse smocking may be needed to avoid the belt becoming overstretched with constant wear. This type of belt makes

The cream and blue silk belts are made by ruching the fabric with random gathering and mounting it over pelmet-weight vilene. The binding is made with matching silk, and the belts have button fastenings.

1 Multiply the waist measurement by three or four (estimating the exact amount as shown earlier, and taking the fastening into account). Cut a strip of fabric to the calculated length by twice the width, plus two seam allowances each way.

Fold the fabric with right sides together and machine stitch along the length, leaving a gap of about 7.5cm (3in.) in the centre. If you are using a very fine fabric, you may need to incorporate a backing of vilene, placing it on the wrong side of the fabric before this is folded and stitched.

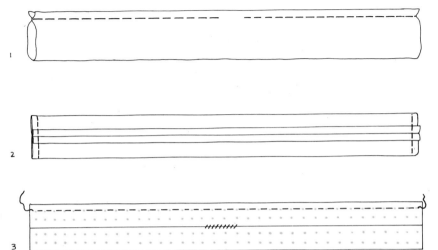

2 Bring the seam allowances out flat and fold the belt so that the seam runs down the centre (back). Stitch across each short end.

Turn the belt right side out, through the gap at the centre of the seam. Push out the corners carefully, then press the belt. Slipstitch the gap in the seam.

3 With the seam at the back, mark the belt with smocking dots and gather it lengthwise. Stitch the smocking design, either taking it right up to the edges or leaving a ruffle at either side. Remove the gathering threads and add an extra piece of binding fabric to carry the buttons, buckle, or other fastening of your choice.

an attractive addition to any daytime wear, or it could be made, using silver lurex threads for the smocking, to wear with a black dress for a very striking evening outfit. Non-elastic belts may be made by stitching the smocked fabric to a backing of heavy-weight vilene interfacing. This can then be finished by placing a lining at the back and binding the edge with matching or contrasting fabric. Alternatively, the smocked piece may be stitched to the vilene, placed face down on the lining, and machine stitched all around, leaving a small gap through which to turn the belt to the right side. The smocking may run along the whole length of the belt, vertically or horizontally, or it may be inserted in the form of panels, set at intervals along the belt, or as a shaped front section.

Ruffles

A delicate smocked ruffle, attached to the front of a blouse or dress, or to a cuff or hem, or, as shown on some of the fashion sketches, down the length of a sleeve, will give a light, dainty look to a garment. The effect will depend on the type of fabric used. Organdie, for example, will make a crisp, erect ruffle, whereas chiffon or voile will produce a much softer ruffle. Whichever effect you require, the fabric should be fine and light so that the ruffle is not too bulky.

If you prepare a double-thickness strip, as for the belt on the previous page, the raw edges will be concealed, but the ruffle will still be light and dainty. If you use a single thickness of fabric, finish the edges with a rolled hem, machine embroidery, or lace, applied before gathering.

Hats

Smocking can be stretched over preformed hat shapes, but there are innumerable other ways in which it can be used, either to add a finishing touch or to create a hat. To make a flower-like decoration for a pillbox hat, for example, gather organdie on a smocking machine, then smock along one edge, making a one-sided ruffle. This can then be folded and manipulated into a flower shape and slip-stitched in place on the hat.

Bonnets for babies and little caps for small children are fun to make. The back section of a bonnet can be smocked and set into a straight strip of fabric which forms the main part of the bonnet, lined and tied with ribbon. To make a frilled bonnet, hem or add lace to the edge of a straight strip of fabric before gathering, and then smock the fabric, leaving the clean edge as a frill. Set the smocked strip into the shaped back section of the bonnet; line it, and add ribbon ties as before. These bonnets can look enchanting when made to match a christening robe.

A mob cap is made by cutting a circle of fabric. The diameter of the circle should be the measurement of the child's head, plus about 8cm (3in.) to allow for a 4cm (1½in.) ruffle all around. Hem or stitch lace to the edge; gather two or three rows about 4cm (1½in.) from the edge, and smock a narrow band around the hat. When the gathers

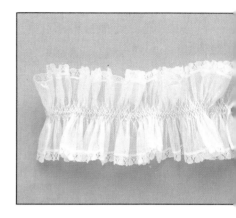

Once the fabric for a ruffle has been prepared and gathered, it is ready for smocking. A minimum of smocking down the centre of the strip – just two or three rows – is all that is needed to hold the gathers and preserve the delicate effect. When the gathering threads have been removed, the ruffle may be slipstitched in place.

Above *If you use small rectangles, made from a single or double thickness of fabric, you can create tiny bows. These make a delightful decoration for clothes, bags or shoes. Try making shoe bows from soft leather, gold kid or ribbon. Measure the size of bow required and make a rectangle to that length, with a width of about half that size. This time, the gathering and smocking runs down the centre, from one long edge to the other, leaving the free ends to spring out in a bow shape.*

Right *This cocktail hat, by Gillian Jenkins, was made by covering a preformed shape with black silk. It was then decorated with tiny frills of organdie, gathered on a smocking machine, using gold threads.*

are removed, the smocking should be sufficiently elastic to hold the hat in place.

A smocked band, beaded and decorated with flowers, makes a charming bridal headdress. Choose the same fabric as the bride's dress and smock a narrow strip in matching threads. Cut a strip of pelmet-weight vilene to size and join the ends together. Stitch the smocked strip to the vilene and add beads, pearls and bullion knot flowers to enhance the smocking. Turn the raw edges behind the vilene; line the band with matching fabric, and attach the veil. Fresh or fabric flowers and ribbons or tiny rouleau strips may be applied to add the final touch.

Bags

Bags come in all shapes and sizes, and in many cases it is possible to incorporate appropriate smocking, designed in proportion to the scale of the bag. For example, smocking on a large scale would be required for a bag made from a heavy-weight fabric, such as sail cloth

Left *Diagonal surface honeycomb stitch over three pleats, stitched with rayon and silk threads, was used for these silk evening bags. For each bag, two squares of smocking were made and cut into crescents. These were joined by a gusset and bound with matching silk.*

Right *To make this bag, Gillian Jenkins dyed silk in soft shades of pink and mauve, and then smocked it with stripes of outline stitch, dividing areas of diagonal stitching over three pleats. Beads were added between the pleats.*

or needlecord. This might be suitable for a beach bag, perhaps with a waterproof lining.

Cotton, linen and many other woven fabrics are suitable for handbags. It is worth considering the use of soft leather, which smocks beautifully, and richer silks, satins and velvets are lovely for evening bags. Allover texture looks very effective: as with clothes, the smocking is stitched first and is then cut to shape.

It is advisable to use an interlining of pelmet-weight vilene, which is flexible and at the same time firm enough to hold the shape of the bag. Finish the edges with binding, or construct the bag with all the seams to the inside.

Fabric handles are easily made. You can choose from a variety of fastenings, including zips, buckles, buttons and loops, or you may like to tie the bag with ribbon or cords. Another possibility is to make a bag to fit a ready-made frame and handle. It is a good idea to look out at sales for antique frames, which are often very pretty and ideal for evening use.

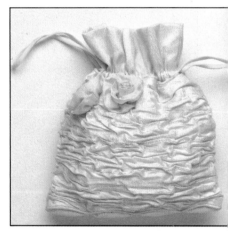

Above *Random gathering was used to ruche the silk for this little drawstring bag, which was then decorated with silk roses.*

Soft furnishings

As with any other form of embroidery, smocking should not be used just for its own sake, but because it achieves the effect you want by fulfilling its original function of controlling gathers in a decorative way. This applies to items in the home as well as to clothes. A nursery decorated with dainty smocked items, or the light ruffled accessories of a young girl's room, are both delightful and practical. The use of smocking in other parts of the house can add the subtle sophistication of texture and colour to the decor.

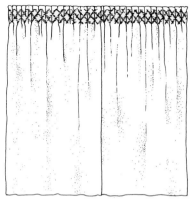

1 Gathered curtain headings lend themselves to smocking, provided the scale is in proportion to the weight of the fabric. For example, thicker threads and larger stitches should be used at the head of velvet curtains, compared to the finer threads and smaller stitches that would be suitable for fine net curtains.

Fabrics dyed in shades of turquoise blue, pink and mauve were used to line the inside of a wooden jewellery box. Inside the lid, Gillian Jenkins has set an embroidered window, edged with smocked, frilled curtains, and tiny bags. The base is padded and has a matching smocked and frilled lavender bag.

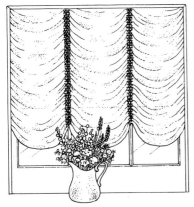

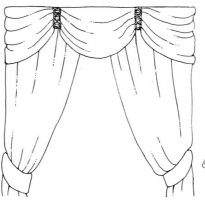

| **2** | Blinds made from semi-sheer fabric, gathered with narrow bands of smocking, make a light, airy window dressing. |

2 Blinds made from semi-sheer fabric, gathered with narrow bands of smocking, make a light, airy window dressing.

3 Pelmets, with inserted panels of smocking – perhaps reverse smocking, for a purely textured effect, or stitched with self-colour threads – can look very elegant.

4 A baby's crib can be draped in the same way, with a canopy and matching ruffle all around. Use plain or delicately patterned fine fabric, stitched in pastel shades and decorated with ribbons.

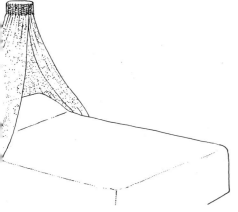

5 A charming canopy can be created by gathering and smocking a band of fine fabric and mounting it on a circle fixed above the bed. If the edges meet at the front, the gathered fabric can be draped softly around the head of the bed, creating a delicate framework and making a focal point.

It may be used on cushions or for curtain headings, as shown overleaf, or perhaps for a soft gathering for a lampshade. The light from a lamp forms a focal point of a room in the evening, and unusual effects are created when the light shines through the varying thicknesses of fabric and stitch patterns formed by a smocked lampshade.

The smocking might be on an even smaller scale – a textured panel set into the lid of a jewellery box, for example. Although there may be many places where you are tempted to gather fabric with smocking, the technique must be used with restraint, as too much smocking may detract from the appearance of your home, making it look busy and fussy.

Cushions

Cushions are often used to reflect aspects of a colour scheme or to add contrast and colour to a room. They offer a splendid opportunity to introduce smocking as an area of texture to contrast with a plain background. An allover texture, created by surface or reverse smocking, is most effective, especially if you add binding, piping, ruffles or lace to finish the outside edge.

A smocked panel inserted into the centre of a cushion, or perhaps set in asymmetrically or diagonally, becomes an important element of the cushion design. The shape of the cushion may dictate the placing of a textured panel, and you may like to consider making a rectangular or triangular shape, as well as the more conventional square. Some of your experimental samples may be suitable for inserted panels. Remember to change the scale of your smocking, if necessary, so that it is suitable for the fabric and in proportion to the whole cushion.

Round cushions and the round ends of bolster cushions are made by smocking a strip of fabric which is about twice as long as the circumference of the finished cushion. As with round necklines, close stitches are used on the inside edge to hold the pleats together firmly, and the more open, elastic stitches towards the outside. The finished smocking is set into a central circle of plain fabric, edged with piping or perhaps lace. The pleats are spread out evenly at the outer edge, and the cushion may be finished with corded piping. Tassels, made with the same threads as those used for the smocking, add an attractive finishing touch to the corners of some cushions or the centre of a bolster end.

Tablecovers

To make a cover for a small table, cut a piece of fabric to fit the table top, and then measure around the edge of the table and cut a strip of fabric three times that length and as deep as the measurement from the top of the table to the floor, plus seam allowances. Gather and smock a narrow band along one edge, and set this evenly into the shaped top of the cover. The gathers will fall prettily from the table to the floor, perhaps echoing the gathers of curtains made in the same fabric.

A set of dainty white pillows, all by Jean Hodges: some contain scented herbs, and each is inset with a panel of smocking in delicate colours, and edged with lace, ribbons and frills.

CHAPTER 5

NEW WAYS WITH SMOCKING

Smocking reassessed

The image of smocking familiar to most people is still that of traditional smocks and children's dresses. This image can be widened by the imaginative use of colour and pattern, and by applying smocking to a variety of objects, but the conventional methods of gathering and stitchery remain the same. The original use of smocking stitches, to make decorative patterns rather than as an interpretative medium, has meant that exploration has been limited by tradition, and until the last few years, the smocking had not kept pace with the exciting expansion of other areas of embroidery.

Classic smocking, with straight, even pleats, beautifully worked with precise stitchery, will always have its place. However, a few people have begun to use smocking in a much more free and creative way, and they have shown the versatility and adaptability of the technique, demonstrating its potential as a way of introducing texture to wall hangings, panels and clothes.

This section of the book is devoted to looking at the new ways of smocking that can be discovered by reassessing the established techniques. These techniques involve both fabric manipulation and stitchery, and the combination of both these processes opens up many possibilities for creating interpretative and tactile surfaces. Each stage should be examined individually, to find more avenues of exploration, and experiments are vital to a better understanding of the craft and for the discovery of new ideas.

Any experimental pieces that you make should be kept as a valuable source of reference. The personal satisfaction of having explored, planned, designed and executed a complete project is far more rewarding than just following a stitch chart and repeating another person's ideas. The suggestions put forward in this section should be regarded as a starting point for your own interpretation, encouraging you to look at smocking in a new light.

Colour fun panels, made from fabric dyed in brilliant reds, blues, pinks and mauve, were smocked, using the lattice pattern and a range of matching threads. The panels were then framed to show the reverse of the pattern and the threads.

88

Fabric creation

Before exploring the stages of smocking, it is worth considering the fabric that you are going to use. Even with the wide range of fabrics available in the shops today, you still may not be able to find the colour, pattern or texture that is right for your project. As you are going to experiment with the technique of smocking, the opportunity to create a new fabric especially for this purpose should not be missed. This is the time to look at the colour schemes you worked out earlier from natural objects, and to consider ways of changing the surface of the fabrics to enhance your smocking experiments. This can be achieved in several ways: by dyeing the fabrics, for example, by machine embroidery, or by applying other fabrics and threads.

Dyes and fabric paints

There is now a wide range of fabric dyes and paints, produced by various manufacturers and made specifically for particular fabrics. They come in the form of powder dyes, liquid paints, crayons or paint sticks, each with a different method of application. Whichever type you choose, it is only necessary to buy the primary colours of red, blue and yellow, with the addition of white and black. From mixes of these basics all other colours are produced by varying the quantities of each colour, adding white to achieve tints, and black to create shades. It is best to prewash all fabrics to prepare them for dyeing, and undyed cotton needs to be boiled to remove any dressing.

Fabric paints

Usually in liquid form, these are intermixable. They can be diluted with water, and are suitable for most fabrics, Pressing with a hot iron or drying with a hair dryer will set the colour permanently. The paints can be applied to dry fabric, to give distinct areas of colour, or to wet fabric, which will make the colours run together and merge. You can use brushes to paint the fabric, or sponges to press the paint into the fabric and produce soft, random areas of colour. Corks, cotton wool buds (Q-tips), and the edges of cardboard will each produce different marks when used for printing on the fabric. Shapes can be printed with natural objects, such as leaves and feathers, or

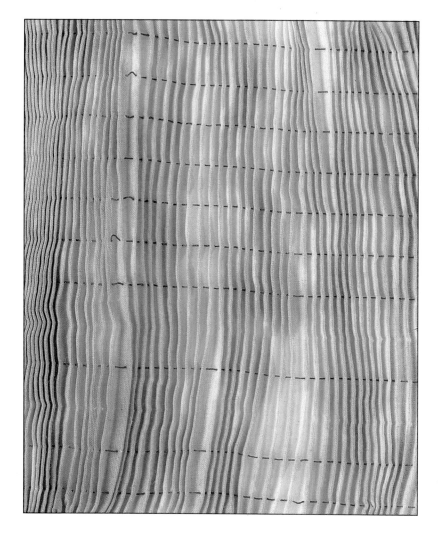

Plain fabric has been gathered and then spray dyed, to create an effect that could be used for rippled water or a summer sky.

you might like to use stencils. Masking tape will cover areas that you do not wish to dye, and you can also make stripes or grids in this way. A speckled effect is made by using a mouth diffuser or air brush. Spray over your stencils or through a grid of canvas or mesh, or vary the density by spraying heavily in one area, then reducing to practically no colour at all. Try gathering the fabric first and then spraying or painting just the edges of the pleats.

Fabric crayons and paint sticks

Use these on fabric just as you would draw on paper, setting the colours with a hot iron. They are useful for drawing lines, grids and more definite shapes, but they will merge into each other if used on wet fabric, and can be overlayed to produce more colours. Try placing the fabric over a rough surface that interests you, such as the bark of a tree or a stone, and use the crayons to take a rubbing, which could form the basis for your smocking design.

Cold-water dyes

These come in powder form and are ideal for dyeing large areas of fabric. They are suitable for most fabrics except pure synthetics; mixtures of natural and synthetic fibres in a fabric will produce an interesting effect when dyed, as the dye is only taken up by the natural fibres. Follow the manufacturer's instructions for normal dyeing. Always add a selection of threads to the fabric in the dye bath, not only to obtain matching tones, but also to help you to build up a good collection of colours for other projects.

Cold-water dyes are also very effective for space dyeing. This is a fascinating, but rather unpredictable method of dyeing, which can

A bark rubbing, made with fabric crayons, can create an interesting background for a smocked design.

create spectacular results, with beautifully merged areas of colour on fabrics and threads. Start by dissolving 100g (4oz) of cooking salt in 600ml (1pt) of hot water, to make a solution that helps to drive the dye into the fabric. Make a similar solution, this time of soda and water, to fix the dye. Lay prewashed pieces of fabric and skeins of thread loosely in a large shallow container or basin. Dry or damp fabric can be used; each will give different results. Choose two or three colours of dye powder, and mix half a teaspoonful of each with a little hot water in separate jars, topping up each jar with salt solution. If you use less dye you will get a paler result; more dye will make a stronger colour.

Taking one colour at a time, spoon the dye on the fabric and threads, spacing the colours out and not overmixing. Leave for ten minutes to allow the dyes to penetrate and the colours to change and merge. Cover the contents with the soda solution and leave for a further 30 minutes to fix the colours. Pour away the dye mixture, then rinse the fabrics and thread thoroughly. Wash in soapy water; rinse again, and allow to dry. You will now have a unique fabric, covered in colours that blend into one another, plus matching threads with which to work a very special smocking design.

This fabric has been space dyed with red, yellow and blue dyes. In some areas, the dyes have merged together, to create yet more colours.

Silk dyes

As with other dyes, the colours of silk dyes will merge when used on wet fabric, and a lovely effect is achieved by sprinkling the wet, dyed silk with salt, which disperses the dye and leaves random areas almost undyed. To ensure that the colours do not run into each other on dry fabric, gutta resist, produced for this purpose, is used to draw a dye-resistant outline around shapes or patterns. The shapes are then filled with colour, which will stay within the outlines.

Transfer dyes and crayons

As the name implies, these are used to paint or draw on paper, which is then placed face down on the fabric and pressed with a hot iron to transfer and set the colour. The dyes can be diluted and are intermixable, and you may be able to use the transfer several times, with the colour fading slightly each time. You may find that you have more control with this method of painting on paper rather than directly on fabric, but it is always advisable to try out samplers with these dyes to obtain the correct colour. Try cutting the painted paper into shapes and use these to print on the fabric, either creating regular patterns or overlaying the shapes, for a more random effect. The crayons can also be overlayed to create more colours, and they are particularly useful for rubbings.

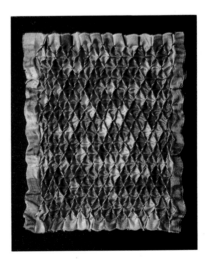

The fabric for Diamond panel *by Mary Fortune was coloured with transfer dyes: a brickwork pattern was painted on graph paper and then ironed on the fabric. Honeycomb stitch was used to form the fabric into diamonds, each a different colour.*

The edges of the stripes, which were made with silk dyes, have been softened by the colours running together.

A much more clearly defined pattern may be made with the use of an outliner resist, as in this sample, in which the colours are contained within rectangular shapes.

Machine embroidery

An ordinary sewing machine will quickly produce stitched texture on a fabric, before it is gathered. Machine lines of straight or zigzag stitches on a plain or dyed fabric. When the fabric is gathered, the lines will run down the front edge of the pleats. The stripes formed by the lines of stitching need not be evenly spaced, and they will catch the light if you use metallic or rayon threads.

A zigzag stitch can also be used to couch down thicker or slubby threads that are laid on the fabric to create lines of texture. Cable stitch can be used to make thicker lines to edge the pleats: wind the bobbin with thick thread, slightly loosening the bottom tension, and work with the right side of the fabric facing down. Alternatively, if you use supple thread in the bobbin and a firm thread at the top, and again loosen the bottom tension, you can make whip stitch, in which bobbin thread is pulled up to the surface and whips over the top thread to make a raised line. Try varying the stitch lengths and the tension, and perhaps use contrasting colours of thread to create different effects. All these methods will make textured lines that will emphasize the front edge of the pleats when they are gathered up.

So far the machine has been used as for normal sewing, but if you remove the presser foot, lower the feed dog, and stretch the fabric tightly over a frame, you will have more freedom. The frame, with the fabric flat against the sewing plate, is moved under the needle while the machine is running, and you can 'draw' with the needle, using either straight or zigzag stitches to make circles, swirls, lines and random patterns, overlaying each other and varying in density. This will cover areas of fabric very effectively and quickly, and by altering the tension, stitch lengths and threads as before, you can achieve great variations of texture. With a little practice, free machine embroidery is soon mastered, and is invaluable for texturing and colouring background fabrics. It can also be used for holding applied fabrics in place. Sheer fabrics, covering interesting threads or unusual scraps or strips of fabric, can also be stitched in this way, producing shadow work embroidery. The rich, colourful and unique fabrics that can be created with free machining will greatly enhance your smocking.

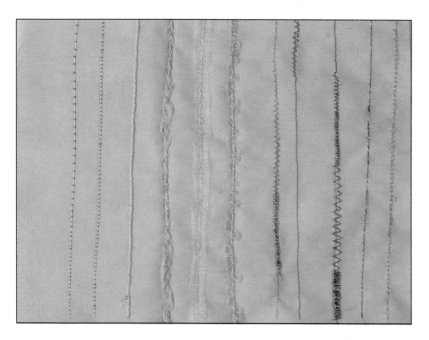

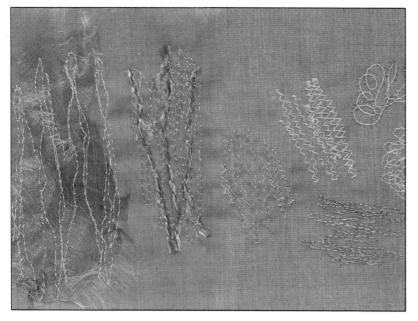

This machine embroidered sample was made with metallic and rayon variegated threads, and shows straight stitch, zigzag stitch in various widths, overlaying textured threads, cable stitch and whip stitch.

Another sample of free machine embroidery, this uses straight and zigzag stitches, overlaying threads and sheer fabrics.

Gathering for texture

The first stage of smocking is the gathering that raises the fabric into folds and pleats, producing the background texture on which the stitches are worked. Traditionally, the smocking dots are placed on the straight grain of the fabric, ensuring that the pleats hang evenly, but if you relax this disciplined approach and experiment with different ways of gathering, you will create fascinating new textures.

If you make up some of the samples illustrated here and on the following pages, you will soon discover how such fabric manipulation experiments can be a source of inspiration for smocking design. It is not necessary to interpret an idea, such as the picture demonstrated overleaf, too literally – the texture of the fabric, the colours and the stitchery should combine to create the image that you wish to convey.

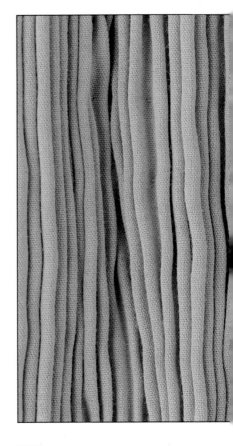

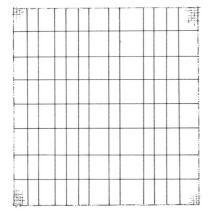

1 Instead of marking the wrong side of the fabric with smocking dots, use air- or water-soluble pens. Again on the wrong side, draw straight lines down the length of the fabric, varying the spacing between lines. Draw lines across the fabric to act as a guide for the rows of gathering stitches.

2 Gather in the normal way, following the lines and picking up one stitch at each point where lines cross. Pull up the gathers and you will now have an interesting surface on the right side, with pleats of variable depth.

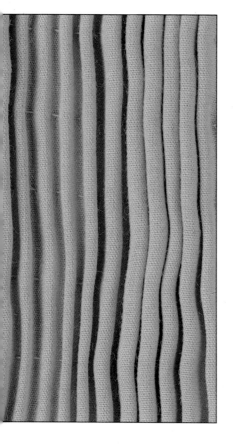

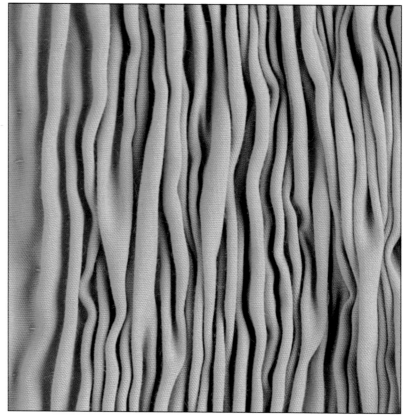

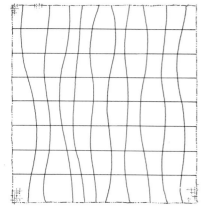

3 Try another sample in the same way, but this time make the lines curve and wave slightly down the length of the fabric, as well as being spaced unevenly.

4 Gather and pull up the threads, as before, this time forming irregular pleats that change depth at random and create a totally different surface. This may suggest a way to interpret grasses, reeds, rock outcroppings or tree bark in an embroidered panel. You might, for instance, make a small picture, like the one overleaf, which depicts reeds growing in water.

Landscapes and perspective

The gathering patterns shown here can act as a starting point for innumerable design ideas. In addition to landscapes, for example, the random groups of lines shown on page 99 would make a stunning surface for the sleeves of an evening jacket.

The linear quality of the pleats can be used to give an impression of perspective. Squeeze the pleats together at one end of a piece of gathered fabric, and spread the other end to make a fan shape. Place the fabric with the wide edge of the fan towards you, and you will see that your eye is drawn along the lines of the pleats towards the narrow end, which could become the horizon of a landscape picture. Dye a piece of fabric to give the impression of a ploughed field, covered with snow, and mark the wrong side in an irregular pattern, as shown in step 1, page 98. Gather the fabric with toning sewing thread and pull up.

Stretch grey background fabric in a frame and place the gathered fabric about two-thirds of the way down. Pull the pleats together at the top and pin them in place. Spread the pleats at the bottom and,

1 Using fabric paints or crayons in several shades of green and brown, paint or draw irregular stripes all over a piece of fabric, merging the colours and stripes into one another.

2 Mark the wrong side of the fabric as shown in step 3 on the preceding page. Gather with green thread, which will blend into the dyed background, then pull up the gathers. Stretch a piece of firm fabric, such as heavy cotton, on a square frame. Lay the gathered piece on the cotton background and manipulate the pleats, spreading them out or pulling them together until you have a pleasing effect. Hold the pleats in place with pins.

when you are satisfied with the position, pin and stitch the whole piece in place.

Use embroidery stitches and knots over and between the pleats in the foreground to convey the feeling of turned earth, stones, roots and plants. Make a line of trees and bushes using hand or free machine embroidery along the top edge of the gathered fabric to indicate the horizon, making sure that the scale is in proportion with the rest of the picture. Remember that at a distance you cannot see any detail of leaves and branches but only the overall shape.

You might enjoy making another landscape, perhaps a field of poppies or buttercups. Choose a blue or pale grey fabric as a background and, using a sponge, daub the fabric with white and grey to suggest clouds. Gather a green fabric – this might be dyed or machine embroidered – following step 2, page 102. Mount this horizontally on the painted background, with the narrow pleats at the horizon. Indicate the flowers, using embroidery stitches and knots, merging them together in the distance and making them brighter, larger and more distinct towards the foreground. These flowers could be made with applied ruched fabric or ribbon.

3 Stitch the gathered fabric to the background. Use either a matching thread and small stitches, which will not show, or toning threads. These might be of various weights, and you might make long straight stitches at random between the pleats, to indicate more reed stems.

4 Choose some shiny threads in a range of blues, whites, greys and silver (space-dyed rayon machine embroidery threads would be ideal for this). Stitch through the pleats at varying depths and spacings across the lower third of the panel, creating an impression of shimmering water.

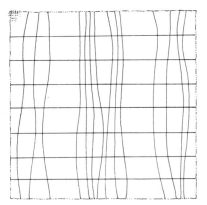  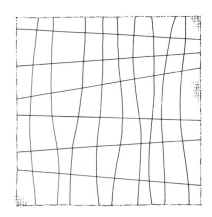

1 Draw varied groups of lines down the fabric and leave different widths of spacing between the groups. Gather each group separately. This will result in groups of raised pleats on the right side, with flat fabric between. The space between the pleats could be covered with rich slubby threads, couched in position, or you might use it for free machine embroidery, hand stitchery, or beading.

2 If you draw lines down the fabric and vary the spacing between them, graduating from a narrow spacing at one side to a wider one at the other, you will end up with graduated pleats, when the fabric has been gathered. Turn the fabric so that the pleats lie horizontally, with the narrow ones at the top, and you will notice a suggestion of perspective, with the pleats appearing smaller in the distance.

3 Mark the gathering lines at different angles, varying the spacing between the gathering lines and the (pleat) lines that cross them. This might form the basis for an abstract panel.

This landscape, using pleats to suggest tree trunks, was made with the gathering design shown in step 1. The pleated areas were painted a dark colour before pleating.

You can create the impression of a snowy ploughed field like this one by dyeing the fabric in appropriate colours and gathering it unevenly, to suggest perspective.

Again, this picture uses a gathering variation and a cross-section of embroidery skills. The flowers could be embroidered, or they could be made with either applied ruched fabric or ribbon.

Abstract designs

In all the samples made so far, the gathering threads have been left in place and toning threads have been used so that they do not show. However, they can be made a feature of the design, providing a contrast between the lines of pleats and the lines of thread. You might, for example, make a large-scale abstract panel, based on a random gathering design, and using an exciting colour scheme. Choose decorative threads and pick up more fabric than usual, so that the threads become an important part of the design. Make some more experimental gathering samples of your own, and think how you would use these to decorate clothes as well as for pictures.

Small pieces of fabric, gathered on a smocking machine, are an excellent way of introducing textured areas into an embroidered panel. If the gathering threads are decorative, they can be left in place, so that the piece can easily be manipulated into shape. Depending on the nature of the design, you might choose to stitch the sample securely in place, using free machine embroidery or by hand, or you might attach it with just a few stitches, leaving the fluted edges free to form part of the design.

In Abstracted landscape *by Sally MacCabe, textured areas are introduced into the panel by gathering pieces of fabric on a smocking machine, manipulating them into shape, and then stitching them on the background to incorporate them into an abstract landscape (photographed by kind permission of Mr and Mrs Jean-Claude Piessel).*

Grid smocking

Gathering used to control fulness, but without surface stitchery, is a form of smocking popular in some European countries. It was developed in an elaborate form in Italy, where the gathering stitches follow a grid pattern, and are worked evenly in and out of the fabric, rather than picking up a small amount of fabric as in English smocking. When the gathering threads are pulled up, the pleats fall into an elaborate symmetrical pattern, quite unlike the straight pleats of traditional English smocking.

Choose a fabric dyed to produce graduated changes of colour, or use beads to emphasize the rippled effect. This method of gathering is easily adapted to much more random and free form designs, which will create fascinating textures and abstract patterns for use on panels or for clothes and accessories. Try your own experiments with this form of gathering to make new textures, thinking all the time how they could be used interpretatively and whether they could be enhanced with the use of dyeing or machine embroidery.

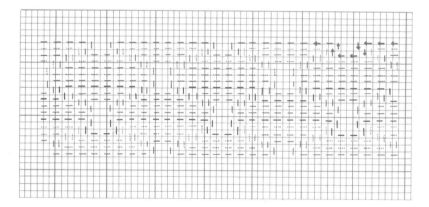

1 Use a strong gathering thread when making up a sample to this grid pattern, based on the Italian style.

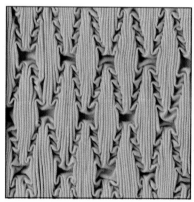

2 When the gathering threads are pulled up, the pleats are bent and distorted into a surface pattern. Patterns of this type, worked out first on a grid, can make a very effective decoration for clothes or for an abstract panel.

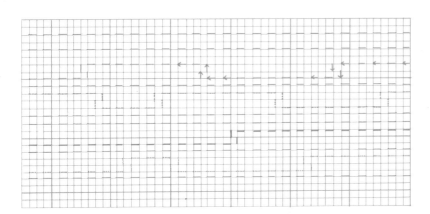

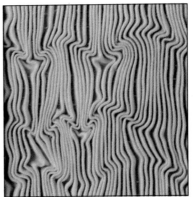

3 This grid is similar to the first, but with changes in direction along the rows.

4 The changes in direction seen on the grid pattern break up the straight line of the pleats and cause a subtly rippled effect across the surface of the smocking. This could be used for an abstract panel, a textured insert at the back of a coat, or as the overall surface of a waistcoat.

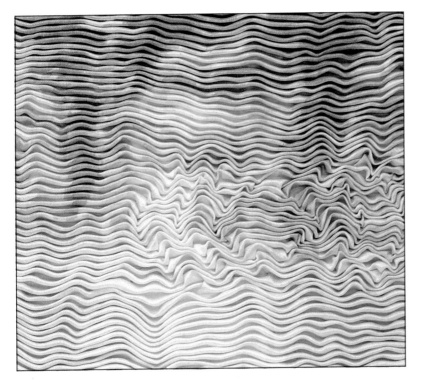

Silk dyes and reverse smocking are here used to create the illusion of fragmented reflections of trees. The circular rippled area suggests a disturbance on the surface of the water, perhaps caused by a fish or a dropped stone.

107

Reverse smocking

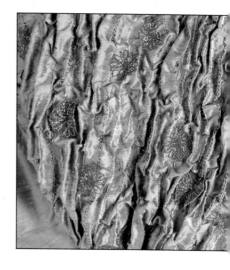

It would be a good idea to build up a collection of experimental samples showing all the methods of gathering. Any of these textured samples could be reverse smocked, if you wish to retain the elasticity of the fabric. Reverse smocking distorts the pleats on the right side into a rippled effect. Outline and cable stitch are most commonly used. They leave a faint line across the surface, but each smocking stitch forms a different pattern of distorted pleats when stretched slightly. If you stretch a piece of reverse smocking really hard, the fabric will bubble up and twist into even more shapes. This property makes reverse smocking an ideal choice for creating abstract texture and surface patterns, which may be used for panels on cushions or for overall texture on clothes. If the stitches used for reverse smocking are used in a more irregular way, then the patterns formed on the surface become more random and subtle, lending themselves to interpreting natural forms, such as the rippled structure of sand at low tide, or the fragmented reflections on the surface of water disturbed by fish or a breeze.

If you take a piece of reverse smocked fabric and bend and manipulate it into curved shapes, you will find that it is extremely flexible and full of possibilities for interpretative designs. The pleats follow each other around in swirls and curves and have an almost fluid quality, which creates a tremendous feeling of movement. This quality can be exploited to depict the flow of water or the movement of wind in grasses, or for a flowing abstract design.

Above and right *The sleeves of this silver grey silk evening jacket are made by first machine embroidering lines down the length of the fabric, using silver thread. The silk is then gathered at random so that the machined lines run along the edge of the pleats. This creates a highly textured surface which is further enhanced by machine embroidered flowers.*

Exploring stitchery

Smocking stitches will look quite different when worked at random or in different directions, or if you vary the scale. The scope for experimenting with smocking stitches is slightly more limited than in the case of other embroidery techniques, because the need to control the pleats restricts the spacing of the stitches. Because the stitches are all worked on the edge of the pleats, there is always some movement of the fabric, and this presents more of a challenge than working on flat fabric. It has the advantage, however, that the pleats become distorted by the stitches, which adds another dimension to the final texture.

At the same time, the wide range of different types of thread can be explored, and by using both thick and thin threads in the same design, or mat and shiny, or smooth and slubby, or flat and round threads, the shape of the stitches can be changed and contrasts are created that will add to the textural interest.

It is a useful exercise, if you have a spare moment, and the energy to use it, to take each smocking stitch in turn and work it in as many different ways as you can: alter the direction or change the scale of stitches in the same row; make the stitches short and fat, long and thin, close together and wide apart; experiment to see if you can distort the pleats in a new way; dovetail or overlap other stitches; work in different weights and textures of thread, or thread the needle with two or three contrasting threads, and use them together.

Transform the regularly spaced zigzags of wave stitch, by working in an unplanned way. Start from any level at the edge of the gathered fabric and stitch across to the other side, making zigzag shapes of different widths and depths, and forming an irregular pattern. Using a different thread, stitch across again, letting some of the zigzags overlap those of the previous row. Continue this process, filling in spaces and building up the pattern until the whole gathered area is covered with the design. Using several weights of thread, and an interesting colour scheme or a range of colour tones, you might equally well decorate a garment or create an abstract panel by using wavestitch experimentally, and trellis stitch can be varied in the same way.

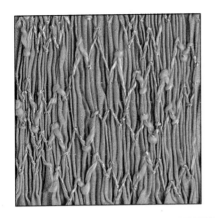

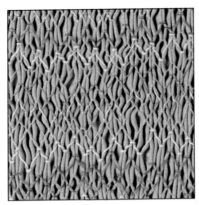

Left and far left *Diamond stitch is a good subject for experiments in random stitching. Stitch the first row at varying levels and with different sizes of zigzag. Form irregular diamonds with the second row, matching the straight stitches at the centre but not mirroring the bottom half of the diamond. Overlay these shapes by making other random diamond stitches, using contrasting textures and colours of thread. Try setting the straight stitches at the top and bottom of the diamonds at an angle, to vary the effect.*

Random wave stitch was used to decorate this child's pinafore dress, which also has blocks of satin stitch at each point, and is stitched with a variety of tones and weights of thread.

Random and diagonal patterns

When the cell-shaped stitches – honeycomb, vandyke and surface honeycomb – are used in a random way, the cells are pulled and distorted into a wide range of irregular and elongated shapes that are wonderfully interpretative. These shapes between the stitches become as important as the stitches in the design, because the shadows formed by their depth contrast with the play of light on the surface.

You might, for example, elongate diamond stitches, taking extra steps until the whole depth of the gathering has been stitched diagonally. If you repeat rows of diagonal stitching, you will find that the pleats are controlled in the same way as when the stitches are worked straight across the gathering, but the pattern created is quite

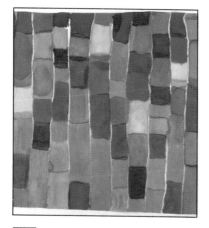

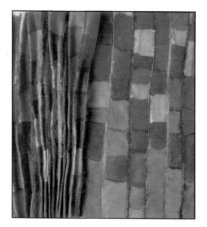

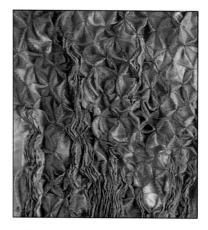

1 To make the honeycomb stitch panel, silk fabric was dyed in a random block pattern, using the bright pinks and purples of the flowers, with bands of green running through at intervals, to represent the leaves and stems. Small pieces of fabric, ribbons and textured threads were dyed at the same time.

2 The textured threads were laid on the fabric between the blocks of colour and machined in place with zigzag stitch and coloured metallic thread. The whole piece was then gathered into relatively large pleats, in such a way that the textured threads were running along the front edges of the pleats.

3 Random honeycomb stitch was used on the pink and purple areas, producing a texture of uneven shapes to indicate the flowers. Each of the green bands of fabric was then regathered separately into much finer pleats, suggesting the stems of the flowers. This process further distorted the fabric, making the flower areas more prominent.

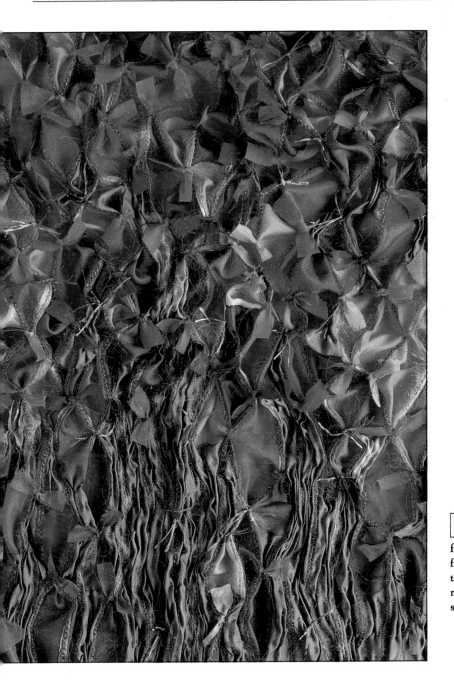

4 The smocked piece was then mounted on a background fabric and stitched in place. The flowers were accentuated by adding tiny bows of fabric, ribbons and raffia over some of the honeycomb stitches.

different. Surface honeycomb and vandyke stitch can also be used diagonally. Contrasting colours will emphasize the diagonal stitchery, drawing the eye down rather than across the smocking.

Double chain stitch, worked over two and three pleats alternately, makes an elongated chain effect. Honeycomb and surface honeycomb, when stitched over three pleats at a time, make the extra pleat twist and distort slightly as the neighbouring pleats are pulled into place by the stitches, creating an interesting addition to the surface pattern. The same is true of vandyke stitch, which, together with surface honeycomb and honeycomb stitches, can successfully be stitched diagonally over three pleats. In this case different pleats are picked up in successive rows, changing the pattern.

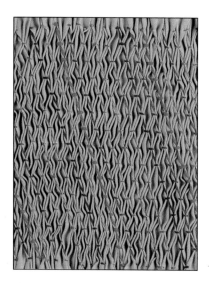

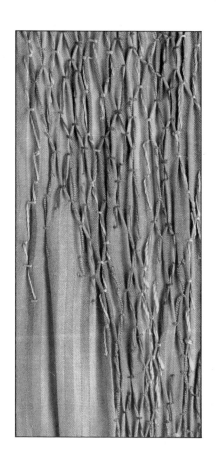

Left *Diagonal surface honeycomb has been stitched over three pleats at a time. The strong, contrasting colours draw the eye down the sample instead of straight across.*

Right *The striped silk fabric was created with space-dyed warp threads and was woven and designed by Lucy Coltman. The colours of the smocking threads echo those of the stripes, and the surface honeycomb stitches are worked down the pleats to emphasize the striped effect.*

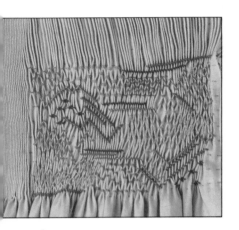

An experimental sample explores the use of several smocking stitches, placed at random rather than straight across the work, dovetailing with each other to create variations of pattern, texture and colur.

Stitch combinations

Like the traditional stitches, experimental variations can be combined with other embroidery stitches and with reverse smocking to make new stitch shapes and pleat patterns. Try covering an area with one stitch, turning the work at the edge of the area and stitching back until the space is filled; then blend in other stitches, dovetailing them to produce a greater variety of pattern texture and colour. Use varied lengths of straight outline or cable stitch, interspersed with the random zigzags of wave stitch and scattered with cable rosettes, or diagonal lines combined with areas of diamond stitch or the random cell shapes of honeycomb. The possibilities for exploring this idea are endless and some inspiration could perhaps be gained from the developments in designer knitwear in recent years. Obviously, far more threads will be used and consequently the starting knots and finishing back stitches will be scattered across the back of the work, but the elasticity can still be maintained if the smocking is to be used for garments. If it is used on a panel or an inserted section that does not need to be elastic, then some threads may be carried loosely a short distance at the back. Look at the back of the work when it is finished, perhaps it will be more exciting than the front?

Surface embroidery stitches can also be used. Raised chain band, which is normally stitched on a grid of straight stitches, can be stitched across the pleats, forming a thick raised line. Needle-weaving stitches produce blocks of colour that contrast well with lighter stitches. Cretan stitch lends itself to smocking very successfully. If you use a variety of threads, colours and stitch sizes, you can create an exciting surface texture. Fly stitch can be used over three pleats and worked downwards, with successive rows overlapping and holding the pleats in place. Think of using tiny stitches and fine threads, or large-scale stitching with thick, textured threads, working the stitches evenly or at random. The permutations are endless, and as you build up a collection of experimental samples, you will know that they are unique to you, because no two people ever work in exactly the same way.

Stitching between the pleats

Instead of using stitches over the pleats to hold them in place, modern smocking artists sometimes fill the space between the pleats. This method does not result in an elastic fabric, because the gathered fabric needs to be mounted on a firm background, stretched on a frame, with decorative stitches used to hold it in place. Below are some ideas with which you might enjoy experimenting.

Straight stitches

Gather a plain fabric with very small pleats, or use a smock gathering machine. Leaving the threads in place, mount the gathered fabric on a background material. Pin the smocking in position so that the pleats are evenly spaced and not too far apart. Mark out your design on the edges of the pleats with an air- or water-soluble pen. Follow the design, using long or short straight stitches lengthwise between the pleats, taking them through to the background material. Use a thicker embroidery thread for the parts of the design that you want to emphasize, and a finer thread for more shadowy areas. The finished panel should resemble a design viewed through fluted glass, with the lines of coloured threads merging with the lines of the pleats to give a slightly out of focus effect. This could be framed as a picture, used to decorate an evening bag, or incorporated into a clothing design.

Couched threads and cords

Again using a plain fabric, which might be dyed or surface-stitched, gather it up evenly or at random, making the pleat size appropriate for the design. Pin it to stretched background fabric, leaving the gathering threads in place. Choose a range of thick threads, smooth and slubby, or twist several finer threads together. Wrap some threads tightly with a finer sewing silk or rayon to make cords. All these, together with the fabric, should build up into an exciting colour scheme, or the piece could be made entirely in shades and tones of one colour to emphasize the texture. Now lay these threads and cords between the pleats, pushing them apart to accommodate one thread or several at a time. Couch the threads and cords in place with single stitches or with blocks of satin stitch.

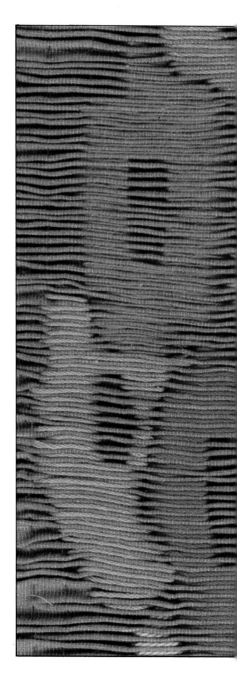

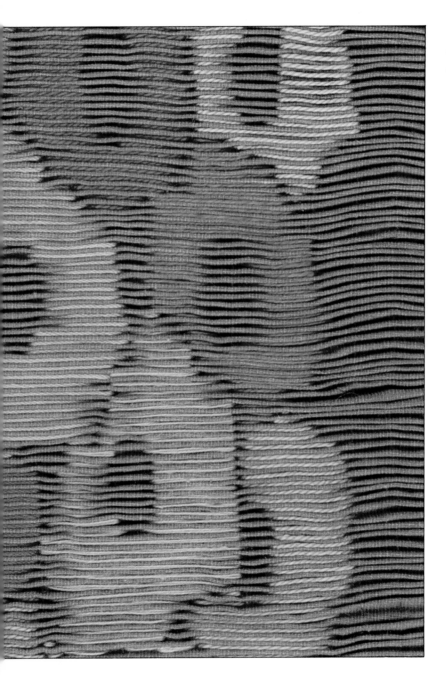

This soft-focus floral group was made by working long straight stitches between the pleats.

Smocking and quilting

Quilting is a technique in which a feeling of movement is easily created by the stitching and by the play of light on the fabric, so it combines well with smocking. Extra fabric is taken up by the wadding in English and trapunto quilting and by cording in Italian quilting, so some of the fulness from the gathers in a piece of smocking may be absorbed into an area of quilting. Stitching used between the pleats might, for example, continue on into quilted shapes, creating a blending and dovetailing of the two techniques. To combine the techniques, work out a design, perhaps one based on the curves of flowing water or the shapes of leaves and flowers, or a landscape. Decide which areas are to be smocked and which quilted, then mark out the areas on the wrong side and dye or surface stitch the fabric where appropriate. Gather up the parts to be smocked separately, evenly or at random, and then, referring to your experimental samples for ideas as to which stitches will achieve the most suitable texture; use reverse smocking or surface stitchery, or stitch and couch between the pleats.

Next, decide which quilting technique to use. English quilting will give an allover padded effect. The whole area to be quilted must be backed with batting and lined with muslin or a fine cotton, and a running stitch is worked through all three layers. If you want to pad selected areas, use trapunto quilting, using the same lining fabric, but no batting. Work the stitching through the two layers to outline the shapes required. Make a small hole or slit in the lining and then gently stuff the shape with small pieces of batting. Italian quilting is also stitched through to a lining fabric, using parallel lines of stitching, through which a cord is passed to make a raised line.

Try to combine the two techniques so that the design naturally flows from one to the other, and finish with surface embroidery and beading if desired. This would be an excellent combination of techniques to apply to clothing.

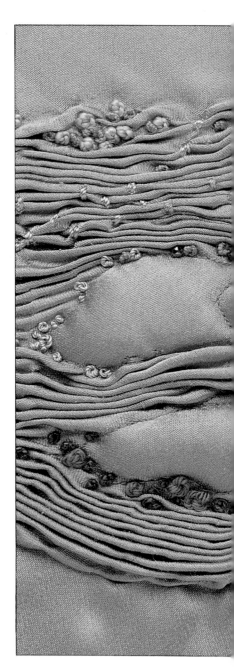

Flowing water around pebbles, created by trapunto quilting for the pebbles and gathered fabric to suggest water.

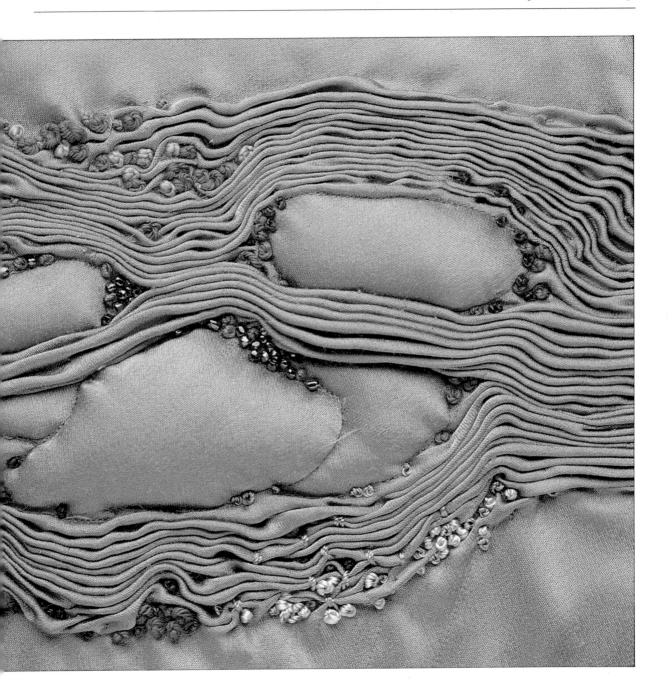

Tucks

It is also possible to smock tucks to achieve a cell-like texture which is not elastic. The tucks may be of even width and spacing or stitched and spaced at random. The flat fabric between the tucks lends itself to decoration with stitchery or applied fabrics and threads. Honeycomb stitch will form even or distorted cell shapes, depending on the placing of the stitches, and the thread can be hidden within the tucks. Other surface stitches, formed with interesting threads, can become a feature if you wrap the edges of the tucks as the stitches are formed.

Explore other embroidery techniques to see if they blend well with smocking, but beware of using too many ideas in one project or of using techniques just for the sake of using them: this results in a busy, over-contrived look. A collection of samples is a useful reference guide when choosing the most appropriate combination of techniques for any new design. Just as the straightforward stitch samples reveal interesting patterns on the reverse side, so the wrong side of

Above *The colours of the striped fabric used for this sample of smocked tucks show up well in the uneven cell shapes created with random honeycomb smocking.*

Left *Reverse lattice pattern smocking is used on the sleeves of this white silk jacket. Bright green threads are used for the smocking and the sleeves are scattered with yellow and white daisies, made by free machine embroidery. Brilliant yellow satin corded piping finishes the edges of the jacket and is also used for the handle of the matching bag.*

The flower pattern shown on page 40 can be varied by altering the sizes of the grids that are picked up and by placing them at random. This gives a more natural look to the texture and is here used to interpret the tiny flowers on a hydrangea blossom. The fabric was dyed, following the lovely range of colours to be found in this flower, and was then pulled up, using a random flower pattern, with some free petals and stitchery added where necessary.

other forms of smocking, such as the lattice pattern, may provide unusual textures. The threads that are normally hidden become a feature on the surface, and the shapes formed are not so regular as on the right side. The square shapes are distorted with slightly twisted corners, and never seem to be an exact repeat of the neighbouring square, however evenly the stitching is worked.

Soft sculpture

Depending on the type and weight of material used, a piece of smocking may be very flexible, with the pleats held together in such a way that the whole piece is almost self-supporting. This makes smocking ideal for creating three-dimensional objects or for soft sculpture. Hold a piece of smocking in your hands and twist, curve, manipulate and mould it to see how it suggests forms and shapes, such as the curves of a shell, the twisted roots of a tree, the meandering of a river, or the arch of pounding waves.

Left and right (detail) *Smocked and padded shapes are used in this three-dimensional panel by Sian Burgess to suggest a variety of bracket fungi and toadstools in a woodland setting. The shapes are stitched to a ruched background and surrounded with leaves and ferns.*

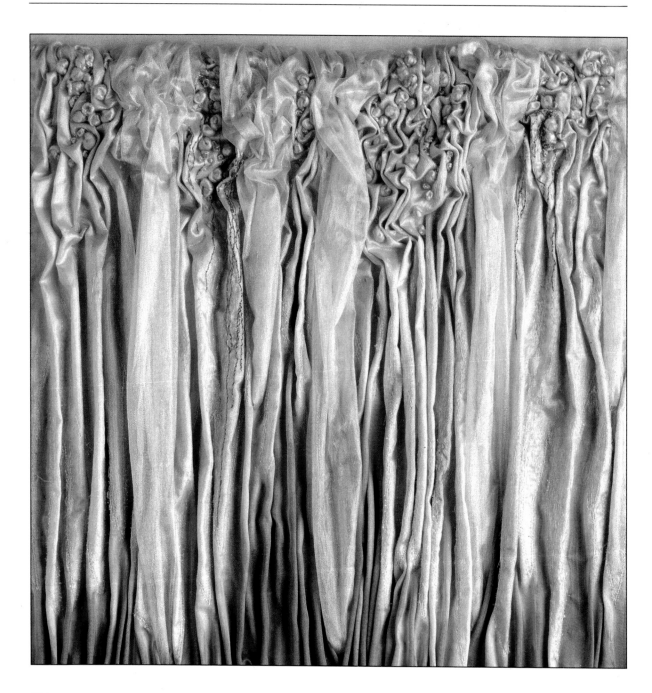

Different surface textures will add to the illusion and will perhaps suggest the skin or fur of an animal, the scales of a fish, the surface of a pineapple or the bark of a tree. Allow the flexibility of the fabric to stimulate your imagination into even more possibilities of interpretation or abstract design. Shape, curve and fold the piece of smocking until it resembles your design, and then stitch it together. Stuff the shape with batting or mount it over a preformed shape or stand. Think of making soft sculptures of people, animals, birds, plants, fruit or vegetables in this way. Perhaps you can achieve the effect you want by overlaying several different pieces of smocking, or by wrapping a cylinder or piece of wood to create the more well defined shape of a building. As with all smocking experiments, it is a matter of giving your imagination free rein.

Far left In Frozen waterfall, *silk fabric was dyed and machine embroidered, then gathered at random and mounted on a background fabric. Pieces of gathered water-coloured fabric were overlayed to suggest the icicles falling from a rock or a frozen waterfall.*

Left Gathered and smocked strips and circles of fabric are manipulated into twisted curving shapes, reminiscent of coral and shells.

INDEX

ACKNOWLEDGMENT

I should like to thank all the embroiderers who kindly lent their work for inclusion in this book. I am also grateful to all those friends for their help and encouragement during the course of the book.

Note: All work is by the author unless otherwise credited.